3

Beyond the Red Carpet

Keys to becoming a successful personal assistant

by

Dionne M. Muhammad

authorHOUSE

1663 LIBERTY DRIVE, SUITE 200
BLOOMINGTON, INDIANA 47403
(800) 839-8640
www.authorhouse.com

First published by AuthorHouse 08/04/04

ISBN: 1-4184-6672-7 (sc)
ISBN: 1-4184-6671-9 (dj)

Library of Congress Control Number: 2004094067

Printed in the United States of America
Bloomington, Indiana

This book is printed on acid-free paper.

Cover Design: *Sharna Joseph*
http://ndoto.home.att.net

Beyond the Red Carpet

Keys to Becoming a Successful
Personal Assistant

Dionne Mahaffey- Muhammad

Acknowledgements

The emergence of this book and my company Celebrity Personal Assistants, Inc. (CPAI) is a gift from ABOVE. I would like to thank my husband Charles Muhammad for his patience and devotion. To our children, Ashanti and Nasir, thanks for understanding when mommy said *"not right now – or – ask your daddy."* Thanks to my mother, Dr. Barbara J. Thomas for teaching me the value of education and giving me your "writing genes." Thanks to my dad, Alvin Mahaffey for the hereditary entrepreneurial spirit. I would like to thank, Gail Hudson, the quintessential celebrity stylist, you have inspired me in more ways than you know; I thank God for people like you, Erica and Miss Juanita. To Corliss Willis, my true friend; thanks for believing in me and for devoting countless hours to help with the growth of CPAI; you are a true sister; may God continue blessing you and your family. Zuheerah Muhammad you are like a mother to me; thanks for your advice and guidance. Thanks to Kristine Hwang, Morris McNeil and Sharna Joseph for Art Direction over the years. To my staff, Nicole Garner, Tamika Howard, Tanya Gray, Tara Parla and Cassandra Brown thanks so much for coming into my life - God always sends us what we need and at the RIGHT time. Argentry Reese — thanks for brotherhood. To my sister, Alva Mahaffey-Johnson, thanks for your creative ideas and vision! Thanks to my business partners Ryan McNeil and Mike Ornstein. Cee Cee Michaela – your ministry is about to explode! Leron E. Rogers, Esq.; thanks for the legal counsel. ☺

Table of Contents

Acknowledgements vii

Introduction.. xi

The Need for Personal Assistants 1
    What Is Your Role? 2
    Types of Assistants... 3
    Production Assistants 6
    What's in a Name? 8

How to get started in a PA Career 11
    Shifting Careers... 13
    Transferable Skills... 13
    Assess Yourself.. 16
    Effective Networking... 18
    Working with Recruiters 21
    Staffing Agencies.. 23
    Job Boards.. 24
    Temp Jobs in Los Angeles 25
    Preparing your Resume 26
    Top Interview Questions 30

Dynamics of the Job... 37
    Partnering with your Employer... 38
    Job Descriptions 40
    A Day in the Life.. 42
    Interview Cheat Sheet... 47
    Characteristics Needed for Success 50
    Appearance 50
    Personality.. 52
    Communication 55
    Adaptability 57
    Mental Agility 59
    Your Health 60
    Speaking Well 61
    Accuracy... 62
    Telephone Courtesy 66
    Sense of Responsibility... 69

Self Improvement 71
Etiquette Tips... 72
World Class Dining 74

Time Management 77
Organizing Yourself to Expand the Time Available 77
Maximizing Your Time... 79

Working in Harmony.. 80
Communicating Effectively with Difficult People 80
Speaking with Confidence and Diplomacy................................ 82
Dealing Effectively with Criticism and Manipulation 83
Preparing Yourself for Criticism.. 83

Growing Professionally.. 84
Personal Computing... 84
Public Relations Savvy... 87
Event Planning... 92
Travel Industry Knowledge.. 93
Security and Logistics 94

Household Management... 98

Concierge Services 99

Appendix A: Author's Picks for *on-the-go* Tools 101

Appendix B: Household Organization Forms............................ 105
Weekly Schedule... 106
Emergency Contact Information 107
Away From Home Checklist.. 108
Daily Diet Tracker 109
Daily To-Do List..110
First Aid Kit Checklist 111
Shopping List...112
Travel Packing Checklist 112
Weekly Menu Planner 113

Appendix C: Further Reading..115

Introduction

When we see our most coveted and beloved stars emerge on television we're only privileged to see the graceful persona they project. Internally we ponder where are their stress lines? Why do they always have flawless hair and make-up? How do they manage to keep it all together? Well, in a world where society upholds unrealistic expectations for celebrities, there is a common bond that keeps these public figures' lives intact: their personal assistant."

For most organizations the most valuable resource is executive performance. Administrative professionals in Corporate America are given the daunting task of keeping their executives' lives on an even keel. The same is true for celebrities. In an industry where "stars" are expected to shine at all times, the professionalism of their personal assistant is paramount.

Beyond the Red Carpet is designed to provide those who hope to enter the personal assistant field with the requisite knowledge to be successful. It will also provide veteran assistants with a continuing education resource to maintain their status in this dynamic industry. It will not focus on tabloid fodder by giving the reader insight into horror stories about the relationship between celebrities and their assistants, nor will it dwell on those assistants whose roles have been reduced to errand runners or gophers. While we understand that some of the menial tasks associated with being an assistant are a part of the job, our mission is to spotlight on the more high-level skills required to effectively manage complex lifestyles. Therefore, we will explore the practical skills you will need *beyond the red carpet* to provide stellar service to your employer on a daily basis. These skills may have already been acquired by some in their corporate roles. We hope to show you how they apply in the private sector when working with an individual instead of a corporation.

Throughout the book, we will pepper the pages with real-world vignettes provided to us by working assistants. For the sake of confidentiality, we have changed their names and have masked the identity of their employers.

The Need for Personal Assistants

The more high-profile a person is whether he is a celebrity, professional athlete, minister, politician, attorney or entertainment executive, the more necessary it is for him to be able to concentrate on performing the most important tasks included in his career. The proper management of his lifestyle can favorably or adversely affect his success and prosperity of his career.

Clearly, the more efficiently and effectively the celebrity performs the important tasks involved in his work, the greater the benefit to his career endeavors and any business enterprises he might own. He should be able to concentrate on those important tasks if he is relieved of some other duties involved in his job; which, while still needing to be performed, can in reality be done by somebody else on his behalf or under his supervision. In other words, the celebrity needs assistance, and that will be provided by at least one assistant.

In this book, we will refer to the personal assistant, lifestyle manager and household administrator by the affectionate title PA. This position requires a one-on-one relationship with the employer. Your role as a PA is that of business manager, confidant, administrative assistant and more. A successful assistant must handle wide-ranging responsibilities and talents. You must have boundless energy and think quickly. In addition to anticipating your employer's whims, it is imperative that you have strong business acumen; diplomacy and political skills; know how to do last-minute decorating construction and labor relations; make travel arrangements; provide public relations expertise; do styling; *and let's not forget* the occasional hand-holding. It is the total, professional delivery of these varied elements to your employer that will help you land and most importantly keep your job as a personal assistant.

What Is Your Role?

Some think the role of an assistant is to walk *toe to toe* with *his* employer down the red carpet; to participate in interviews on *Access Hollywood* or *Entertainment Tonight* and to become his employer's best friend and enjoy the perks that are stereotypically associated with being a celebrity. Others feel it is a position for sycophants and errand runners who go and get newspapers and scoop the dog poop from the front lawn. Both the former and latter are at face value wrong.

The PA's role is about leadership. The PA takes responsibility for much of the organization and coordination of his employer's lifestyle and business needs. It is a task that calls for tact, diplomacy and effective communication and organizational skills. A good PA makes an enormous contribution to his employer's effectiveness and requires numerous professional skills to be successful in this role. Today's PA must be "the barber, the baker and the candlestick maker." Most often there is nothing new an experienced corporate professional must learn to get the job done. For example, things learned in any corporate environment such as computer skills, project management, customer service and strategic planning can all be repurposed for working as a PA. However, adaptation is needed when it comes to working in the environment of a high-profile person. One must dispose of the 9:00 a.m. to 5:00 p.m. mindset and quickly become accustomed to being on call twenty four hours a day. In some cases, there is no time to cultivate a "personal life" for yourself; some assistants admit that they have no friends, no love life and are too busy to even take care of a plant. While this is not the case for all assistants, you must carefully consider the environment and work ethic of the person you will be assisting before accepting a position as his PA.

Types of Assistants

Job openings, like job applicants, are not all the same. The personal assistant is concerned with communicating information between the employer and the people and entities in the employer's life.

Executive Personal Assistant:
The executive personal assistant's salary ranges from $60,000 to $130,000 per year. These assistants usually support A-list actors, producers, music executives, and investment bankers. They support their employer with high level tasks outside the home and professional business skills are necessary. Often seen as the life support machines of their employer, these senior PA's are a hybrid of project manager, secretary, and confidant to the employer. They are given more responsibility, autonomy and recognition. Beyond the typical administrative requirements, there are certain key attributes and skills that set these PA's apart:

- high level business acumen
- PR and communication skills

- flexibility and initiative
- ability to manage projects
- intuition and empathy
- commitment to the organization
- working 'beyond the job description'

Gate-keeping - adding value - and going beyond the call of duty are just some of the attributes required at the "executive" PA level. To succeed, a PA needs to be totally prepared to go that extra mile. They must be able to deal with all aspects of business life from working with a team, to supervising projects, to organizing events and managing budgets. They must be persuasive communicators with a level of business insight previously required only in corporate middle-management positions. These days, celebrities prefer PAs that are polished, career-focused professionals with a solid career history. In one-to-one relationships, knowing what your employer needs and understanding his career goals are essential requirements. Responsibility and trust increase the longer you are with the employer. Ultimately, as a right-hand person, the more work you can take away from your employer, the greater the value you add.

"You're not talking about a girl-Friday anymore. You're talking about a well-educated, well-spoken person who acts as an alter ego," said **Argentry Reese**, a private accountant to professional athletes. "You're paying someone to represent you. Therefore, they must offer more than lowly gopher and errand services."

In a 2003 *Herald Tribune* article, Tampa Bay Buccaneers head coach, Jon Gruden said of his assistant, "He helps me with every facet of my life, from an organizational standpoint," Gruden said. "I think he understands me probably as well as anyone in my life right now. He really helps me to be as efficient as I can." Titled as the assistant to the head coach, Mark Arteaga is Gruden's jack-of-all-trades, sounding board, confidant, valet, right-hand man, advisor — you name it.

Personal Assistant/Household Administrator:

A domestic personal assistant's approximate salary ranges from $35,000 to $80,000 per year. These assistants work directly with the employer and can also be of service to the house manager, butler, or major-domo. Duties could include care of house guests' needs and requests, coordination of parties and other events, personal shopping, handling of personal correspondence, keeping the family calendar and appointments, and being an expert at proper table and household decor.

Below are other positions that share similar
domestic responsibilities of a PA:

Butler: Approximate Salary Range: $45,000 to $100,000 per year. Butlers are formally trained and highly experienced. They supervise and coordinate activities of the household and all household employees. They receive and announce guests, answer the telephone, set the table, serve meals and drinks, and perform various personal services.

Major Domo: Approximate Salary Range: $85,000 to $225,000 per year. Major-Domos' are responsible for the care of an estate or estates. They usually have the responsibility for the inside care of the estate. Employers rely on them to provide continuity of staff, service and personal needs between all properties. Their duties might also include managing financial accounts, seasonal opening and closing of employer's estates, and acting as a personal assistant.

House Manager: Approximate Salary Range: $35,000 to $60,000 per year. House Managers must be experienced in the daily running of a household. Duties could include managing a staff, housekeeping, laundry, ironing, errands, grocery shopping, cooking, or basically whatever needs to be done.

Production Assistants

Production Assistants are also called PAs and they have some of the same responsibilities as a personal assistant. They **must** also possess **technical** knowledge of film or television production. They play a key role in ensuring that the production runs smoothly, i.e. that the program is produced on time and within budget. They provide administrative support to the producer and director and are involved in all stages of the production process from pre-production through to post production. The production assistant's role varies depending on the nature of the production. This could be a live show or drama production, which is based in a studio or on location. One of the key roles is to ensure the program runs to time, to the split second in many cases. A production assistant is involved with a program from the outset.

Typical work activities include:

- co-coordinating and communicating the production resources and facility arrangements;
- checking copyright issues and ensuring royalties are paid;
- attending and co-coordinating planning meetings;
- undertaking preliminary research for the program;
- cueing or playing pre-recorded material;
- giving advice and support to presenters and other members of the production team;
- producing timing schedules;
- liaising between producer/director, technical team and presenters;
- budgeting;
- planning activities;
- booking performers;
- organizing the production and distribution of all scripts;

- attending to logistics, such as contracts with external organizations, schedules, catering and accommodation for performers and crew;
- anticipating situations and acting/advising appropriately;
- monitoring and timing during the shoot;
- ensuring continuity on location and keeping accurate shot lists, especially for drama productions;
- dealing with artist payments and expenses;
- acting as the liaison between the producer and the post production team.

What's in a Name?

Although the term "personal assistant' or PA has been in use for many years, it has been very much more common for such an assistant to be referred to as a 'secretary; or as a 'private secretary.' However, over the years, the word secretary has gradually come to be used as a generalized description of many different people who perform work in an office environment. Although the work they perform might vary considerably from organization to organization; in general, it is of a clerical nature. Indeed, many of those concerned are, in reality, no more than office clerks – although perhaps senior experienced ones – and they are given the courtesy or honorary title of secretary or administrative assistant.

Similarly, many office personnel who are actually receptionists or other clerical or administrative roles might be referred to as "assistants." This trend of using more dignified titles can be seen in other fields as well; for example garbage men are now often referred to as "refuse collectors."

In recognition of the increasingly important roles played in many companies by assistants to executives, the descriptions "administrative assistant" and "executive assistant" are being used far more often today and it is likely that the trend will accelerate. We cannot, of course, say what descriptions you will come across – or be designated – during your career, and circumstances differ from country to country and from enterprise to enterprise.

In the private sector, when working with celebrities, the designation "personal assistant" is used; or for simplicity, the title PA is applied. But when we use this title in our agency and in this book we shall be referring to a person who is a specialist at lifestyle management. These PA's are aware that the busy lives of celebrities require Personal Assistants to be not only extremely efficient and reliable, but flexible in their responsibilities and schedule. The candidates placed by Celebrity Personal Assistants, Inc. are given the job title Lifestyle Manager and we hope that as in the corporate sector how the name has evolved from girl-Friday to clerk to secretary to administrative assistant – we hope that PA's will soon enjoy a more befitting title that captures the essence of the services they provide – lifestyle management.

Probably the majority of personal assistants are female, but there are many who are male; merely for convenience the words "she" and "her" are often used when referring to a PA - instead of the rather cumbersome expressions "he or she" and "his or her." Merely for the sake of convenience the words "he" and "his" and "him" are used when referring to the executive or celebrity.

How to get started in a PA Career

A job search is a sales campaign - and the product is you. As a corporate professional you have written business plans, developed marketing strategies, sold and closed deals. That is precisely the process you should follow to define, pursue and change careers to land a top job as a Personal Assistant. Below is an outline of a sample "Career Plan" aspiring PAs can follow:

1. **Choose the type of Employer**: Musicians or actors are not the only individuals who need personal assistants. Personal Assistants can work for professional athletes, attorneys, sports agents, politicians, directors, bestselling authors, affluent families, basically anyone with enough wealth can hire someone to manage their complex lifestyle.

2. **Organize your Job Search:** Juggle cover letters, resumes, follow-up calls, appointments, interviews and thank you notes with all the right tools. Build the perfect resume that works in all the applications you'll use for your on-line and off-line job search.

3. **Enhance your Skills**: Personal Assistants need to know a little bit about everything, and know where to find out more. The ability to be resourceful is vital. PAs must be able to find "any type of information" at any time. Most affluent employers are looking for savvy, technologically competent employees who can show them

11

how to transfer information from their palm pilot to the computer or keep track of their personal finances.

4. **Take Courses:** Computer training, project management and other administrative courses are necessary for today's professional personal assistant. Classes offered by butler schools and other domestic training institutions can also serve as an education resource. Investigate part-time training, distance learning and online courses. Doing training in your own time shows commitment and will help convince future employers that this was a decision you thought about carefully and then followed through.

5. **Expand your Career Network:** Create and utilize a powerful set of industry contacts - people who know the industry and can provide you with leads and unpublished opportunities. Tap the hidden job market by building relationships with recruiters - they often have the direct line right to opportunities and make sure that your resume gets into the hands of the right people. **Networking is an important first step:** Let everyone know that you are a Personal Assistant looking for work. Contact a celebrity directly by getting in touch with their publicist, agent or business manager; or contact a staffing agency like CPAI or an organization for working personal assistants such as the New York Association of Celebrity Assistants or the Los Angeles based Association of Personal Assistants.

6. **Get Hired:** Nail the interview, follow-up, follow-through, and negotiate the best employment package.

Shifting Careers

So, you've been a corporate banker all your life but *now* you want to be a personal assistant. Changing jobs is tricky enough, but shifting careers is another matter. We're all used to the idea that no job is for life and many of us move frequently between employers with relative ease. But changing careers completely is a bigger and much more complex decision - and one a lot of aspiring personal assistants are grappling with.

Being in one job for a long time – or out of work for a while can make you believe there's not much you're good at, apart from what you're already doing. If you let yourself fall into that trap, the rut you're in will feel deeper than it really is. There are so many skilled things we do instinctively every day that we stop recognizing them as special. Many of these things are proficiencies personal assistants need in order to be successful. Knowing you are skilled and capable gives you the confidence to try new things. But how easy do you find it to see just how good you are and then describe that to someone else?

Transferable Skills

Finding a personal assistant job doesn't have to be difficult. Qualifications and experience aside there are some very important attributes that all employers feel they can't get enough of:

- Communicating effectively
- Working well in a team
- Problem solving

- Using initiative
- Being well organized
- Being adaptable

These transferable skills are essential for success in the most high-powered jobs. Yet they are often learned and perfected in ordinary situations. Ironically, many of us completely overlook our abilities just because of that.

CASE STUDY: Candice had been a customer support representative before taking a two year break to care for her sick mother. After her mother died she confided in a friend that she was interested in returning to work, but did not want to go back to a "desk job." Her friend suggested that she try her hand at personal assisting. Candice quickly replied, *"I have never done that – and am not qualified to work with celebrities."*

Her friend took the liberty of writing a resume for Candice. She was sure to include important key words that would get the attention of employers and recruiters. She structured Candice's resume using bullet points to ensure that the important talents would stand-out. Through some creative networking on her friend's part, Candice was invited in for an interview with a music producer. Prior to the interview, her friend helped her create a profile of herself that concentrated on the personal skills she had gained during her two year's of caring for her mother; (running errands, scheduling doctors appointments, managing her parents household, paying bills, corresponding with doctors and insurance representatives, etc.). Candice used her professional skills to help settle the estate and deal with other important matters related to her mothers finances.

"Once I realized that the skills that I learned in my previous jobs were needed by the producer I was interviewing with – my confidence level grew ten-fold. I'd been doing superb lifestyle management for the last two years. It paid off; he hired me on the spot."

Assess Yourself

Candice's experience and tactics can be adapted to any situation. Do an audit of your own skills by thinking how the things you do every day can provide proof of how skilled you are. The checklist below should get you started.

Re-evaluate yourself

I'm an effective communicator because I can:

- speak clearly and accurately
- talk easily to strangers
- listen carefully
- persuade others of my point of view
- follow written instructions
- ask the right questions
- explain things effectively
- reach agreement by negotiating or bargaining

I'm a good team-member because I:

- get along well with all sorts of people
- share information
- am open to other people's ideas
- am loyal
- trust others
- am flexible and prepared to compromise
- deliver what I promise
- always support team mates by doing my fair share

I'm a problem solver because I can:

- see problems before they get too big
- look at difficulties from different points of view
- tackle things myself rather than leaving it to someone else
- learn from my own mistakes
- try out new solutions

I show initiative all the time because I'm:

- able to see what needs doing without being told
- willing to take on new things
- good at making decisions
- good at getting things started

My organizational skills mean I'm:

- able to plan work so that the most important things get done first
- able to get things done on time
- good at doing more than one thing at a time
- good at planning how things should be done
- able to co-ordinate people and resources

I'm adaptable because I'm:

- open to new ideas
- not afraid to try different ways of doing things
- quick to learn new things
- able to deal with changes

Dionne M. Muhammad

Effective Networking

Most personal assistant jobs are part of the hidden or unadvertised job market. The unspoken rule in show biz is: "it's who you know." The truth is most jobs go to friends, or friends of friends or family members, or friends of family members. But if you know the right people you will make contacts!

If you tend to be outgoing and are comfortable with contacting new people, you can spend time networking your way to one of these dream jobs. Traditional networking involves developing a list of your personal and professional contacts, informing them that you are conducting a job search, and asking your contacts to point you in the direction of anyone they know in the industry who may be able to help. Once you determine *who knows whom*, ask them to write a letter of reference for you. Most celebrities prefer direct referrals from someone they know, so it is imperative that you tell *everyone that you know* to tell *everyone they know* you are looking for a job. The key to effective networking is to let all of your contacts — and those contacts to whom you are subsequently referred — off the hook with regard to knowing about a specific job opening (in writing and verbally). You are only hoping for further contacts who may not necessarily know of a job opening, but who may be able to "point you in the direction" of someone who also may or may not know of a job opening. People are far more open to helping and referring when they realize you are not expecting them or their referrals to know of a specific job opening at the time.

Once you have your rolodex filled you should start **marketing** yourself by mailing, e-mailing, or faxing *personalized letters and résumés* to decision makers.

This strategy is different from the less effective traditional strategy of mass mailing letters and résumés to *generic* recipients like "Human Resources Department" or "Hiring Manager," which we do not recommend. Take a straightforward approach with regard to the fact that you are looking for a job. Names of key decision makers in a celebrity's life are also sometimes available on the Internet; if not, they are published in various print directories, often from the same source as their online counterparts (ask the reference librarian at your local library). You can do a search for a celebrity's publicist, attorney, agent, business manager, etc.

After identifying the decision maker, personalize and send your cover letter and résumé to this person. Although in the traditional job search you should follow up after each mailing with a telephone call to the recipient; that is not recommended when working with celebrities. You do not want to be viewed as a star-struck. Your motive for sending the resumes and letters is for "branding" you simply want to end up in a decision maker's file for any upcoming openings.

However, if one of your personal contacts suggests or arranges for you to make a phone call to a decision maker, make sure to do so.

Although you will want to put it in your own words, the following is an example presentation for your telephone contact:

Dionne M. Muhammad

•Introduction: "Good morning Mr. Jones. My name is Pat Smith. I am an experienced project manager with an in-depth knowledge of getting things done on time and within budget. I am interested in transferring those skills to a role as a personal assistant. Have I caught you at a good time? ..." [Unless you hear a definite no, follow immediately with a brief professional profile]

•Create interest with a brief professional profile: "... I have most recently been involved with developing ..." "I think I can bring value to *<Add Celebrity's name>* because I am detail oriented ... flexible..."

•Clarify purpose—forward conversation: "...The reason I am calling is that I am looking for a new challenge and, having researched some of the people you represent, I felt we might have some areas for discussion, or at least you might be able to point me in the right direction. Are these the kinds of skills you look for in a prospective personal assistant?"

If the decision maker knows of an upcoming or current opening, typically questions will be asked regarding your background. If there does not seem to be a current interest, you will want to obtain a referral to another decision maker who may or may not have a current opening. Of course, a secondary objective is to remain in this decision maker's personal file for future openings.

•To obtain a referral you might say something like: "Mr. Jones [or use first name if appropriate], whom else might you know — who may or may not necessarily have an opening — but who might be able to point me in the right direction? ... [If so] May I use your name?"

It is a good idea to send a thank-you card, note, or e-mail to those contacts who have referred you to others. You can take this a step further and update your contacts with a note or e-mail when you obtain a position. With this process you are building a professional network targeted toward industries and organizations of interest. This network can serve you now and in the future.

Working with Recruiters

It is a growing trend that celebrities are using staffing agencies (such as Celebrity Personal Assistants, Inc.) to find their assistants. Personal Assistants are expected to be more business savvy these days and structured human resources is a perfect medium for finding someone to manage a celebrity's lifestyle. When approaching staffing agencies, it is best to know in advance how recruiters operate. Recruiters are aware that the busy and demanding lifestyles of high profile employers require Personal Assistants to be not only extremely efficient and reliable, but flexible in their responsibilities and schedule. That is why most search firms specialize in the Training and Developing of MULTI-FUNCTIONAL Personal Assistants who are skilled in a number of different fields and adaptable in their working environment. Before you try to reach recruiters, the following tips on how to make yourself more appealing may be helpful:

Contact search firms that specialize in Personal Assistant staffing. Generate a list of your key requirements for a new position and then identify firms that fit these parameters.

Seek networking contacts who can arrange personal introductions to recruiters. They will be more likely to take the call when [you're] referred to them by someone they know or to do a client a favor.

Be good at what you do. Excel at your job, perhaps by volunteering for extra assignments. Volunteering is important if you are making a career change. Perhaps you can volunteer at a celebrity-themed event (charity event; golf tournament; food-drive). This will add more "gloss" to your resume and show that you are somewhat familiar with the entertainment and sports industry.

Use the channels to reach recruiters. Many search firms are soliciting resumes on their Web sites. For the first time in their business, they are inviting a dialogue with active job hunters by accepting resumes through their Web sites. In other words, the door used to be closed unless they called you. Now there's a way through the door. Their ads may not disclose the name of the celebrity they are hiring for, but they describe real openings. Your chances to land a position will be greater if you do not have a "specific" celebrity in mind. Besides, most recruiters shy away from people that list "I want to work for <Celebrity Name> only.

Be helpful to recruiters. Do not apply for positions that you are not qualified for; recruiters call this SPAM. If the job advertisement states specific requirements that the candidate must have – then only applicants that fit the bill should submit their resume. Await a call from a recruiter. They are hired by their clients to find ideal candidates and you should understand that they will call you if you are what they are seeking. When applicants deviate from the suggested application process, recruiters view this as an inability to follow instructions and usually delete these type of candidates from their databases. They would rather not risk sending a candidate that can't follow instructions to a client for consideration.

Staffing Agencies

Below are agencies that often list positions for Personal Assistant positions. These job openings span all genres of high-profile individuals, including athletes, celebrities, business executives, real-estate moguls, authors, organizations and wealthy families. Aspiring PAs should register with at least 5 agencies to increase their chances of placement.

Celebrity Personal Assistants, Inc.
http://www.celebritypersonalassistants.com

Distinguished Domestics
http://www.distinguisheddomestics.com

Domestic Placement Network
http://www.dpnonline.com

Kerri Campos Inc.
http://www.kerricampos.com

Pavillion Agency

http://www.pavillionagency.com

Professional Domestic Services

http://www.professionaldomestics.com

Sterling Domestics

http://www.sterlingny.com

Job Boards

In addition to agencies, online job boards are a great resource for finding PA jobs.

Show Biz Jobs

http://www.showbizjobs.com/

Entertainment Careers

http://www.entertainmentcareers.net/

Craig's List

http://www.craigslist.org/

Animation World Network

http://www.awn.com/

Employ Now

http://www.employnow.com/

Media Bistro

http://www.mediabistro.com/

Temp Jobs in Los Angeles

Apple One, Glendale

818-241-6002

(Disney, NBC, Warner Bros)

Ultimate Staffing, Century City

310-201-0062

(Fox)

Star Personnel, Beverly Hills

310-278-8630

(Paramount Studios and Talent Agencies)

Venturi Staffing, Los Angeles

323-931-9400

(Paramount Studios and E! Entertainment)

The Right Connections, Los Angeles

310.657.3700

(Disney)

Preparing your Resume

Describing your work experience isn't easy. The majority of those seeking employment as a personal assistant these days have never worked in the role. Many question how their past work experience will be attractive to potential employers. To help, we've compiled a list of power verbs and keywords that will make your resume a standout no matter what type of job you are seeking.

The purpose of using key words and power verbs is to show employers and recruiters that you know how to get results. Begin your job descriptions with a power verb or phrase: enlisted the support…, formed a committee…, sold, budgeted, improved, increased, maintained the client relationship.

A-B

accelerated acclimated accompanied accomplished achieved acquired acted activated actuated adapted added addressed adhered adjusted administered admitted adopted advanced advertised advised advocated aided aired affected allocated altered amended amplified analyzed answered anticipated appointed appraised approached approved arbitrated arranged ascertained asked assembled assigned assumed assessed assisted attained attracted audited augmented authored authorized automated awarded avail balanced bargained borrowed bought broadened budgeted built

C

calculated canvassed capitalized captured carried out cast cataloged centralized challenged chaired changed channeled charted checked chose circulated clarified classified cleared closed co-authored cold called collaborated collected combined commissioned committed communicated compared compiled complied completed composed computed conceived conceptualized concluded condensed conducted conferred consolidated constructed consulted contracted contrasted contributed contrived controlled converted convinced coordinated corrected corresponded counseled counted created critiqued cultivated cut

D

debugged decided decentralized decreased deferred defined delegated delivered demonstrated depreciated described designated designed determined developed devised devoted diagrammed directed disclosed discounted discovered dispatched displayed dissembled distinguished distributed diversified divested documented doubled drafted

E

earned eased edited effected elected eliminated employed enabled encouraged endorsed enforced engaged engineered enhanced enlarged enriched entered entertained established estimated evaluated examined exceeded exchanged executed exempted exercised expanded expedited explained exposed extended extracted extrapolated

F-H

facilitated familiarized fashioned fielded figured financed fit focused forecasted formalized formed formulated fortified found founded framed fulfilled functioned furnished gained gathered gauged gave generated governed graded granted greeted grouped guided handled headed hired hosted

I

identified illustrated illuminated implemented improved improvised inaugurated indoctrinated increased incurred induced influenced informed initiated innovated inquired inspected inspired installed instigated instilled instituted instructed insured interfaced interpreted interviewed introduced invented inventoried invested investigated invited involved isolated issued

J-M

joined judged launched lectured led lightened liquidated litigated lobbied localized located maintained managed mapped marketed maximized measured mediated merchandised merged met minimized modeled moderated modernized modified monitored motivated moved multiplied

N-O

named narrated negotiated noticed nurtured observed obtained offered offset opened operated orchestrated ordered organized oriented originated overhauled oversaw

P

paid participated passed patterned penalized perceived performed permitted persuaded phased out pinpointed pioneered placed planned polled prepared presented preserved presided prevented priced printed prioritized probed processed procured produced profiled programmed projected promoted prompted proposed proved provided publicized published purchased pursued

Q-R

quantified quoted raised ranked rated reacted read received recommended reconciled recorded recovered recruited rectified redesigned reduced referred refined regained regulated rehabilitated reinforced reinstated rejected related remedied remodeled renegotiated reorganized replaced repaired reported represented requested researched resolved responded restored restructured resulted retained retrieved revamped revealed reversed reviewed revised revitalized rewarded routed

S

safeguarded salvaged saved scheduled screened secured segmented selected sent separated served serviced settled shaped shortened showed shrank signed simplified sold solved spearheaded specified speculated spoke spread stabilized staffed staged standardized steered stimulated strategized streamlined strengthened stressed structured studied submitted substantiated substituted suggested summarized superseded supervised supplied supported surpassed surveyed synchronized synthesized systematized

T-W

tabulated tailored targeted taught terminated tested testified tightened took traced traded trained transacted transferred transformed translated transported traveled treated tripled uncovered undertook unified united updated upgraded used utilized validated valued verified viewed visited weighed welcomed widened witnessed won worked wrote

Top Interview Questions

Going for an interview? We profiled several high-profile celebrities and recruiters. They revealed some of the more testing questions they ask and, more importantly, what they look for in your answers.

Why do you want to be a Personal Assistant?

Why they ask it: They want to know if you are a 'career PA', which is what employers typically want, rather than someone trying to get a foot in the door to move onto other areas. They also want to make sure you are not star-struck.

Example of a good answer: "I like providing support to someone. I enjoy organizing, am willing to learn, am flexible, and seek variety in a role. I would also like to make use of the skills I learned in college."

A poor answer would be: "Because it's a good stepping stone into this industry." - or - "Because I love being around celebrities."

Describe a time when you were faced with a number of tasks, all of which needed to be completed in a very short period, some of which were interesting and some weren't.

Why: This shows the employer a number of things: if the candidate is good at time management, for example, and how good they are at prioritizing. It also offers insight into the candidate's character. If it is not an interesting task, will they still treat it with the importance it deserves?

Example of a good answer: "I often had to juggle different tasks at the same time in my previous role (provide actual examples). It is always difficult in a job to be motivated to work on tasks that don't interest you, but I always found that the best way to handle this was to prioritize according to how critical each task was, and work from there rather than an angle of interest or boredom."

A poor answer would be: "I always do the most interesting jobs first and, when these are done, I will move onto the boring ones."

You realize you are not going to finish your workload to an important deadline. What do you do?

Why: This gauges the candidate's ability to understand deadlines, and whether he or she is forward-thinking, able to remain calm and prepared to ask for help when required.

Example of a good answer: "I would speak to my boss, and explain that I am not going to get the work finished, as it is taking longer than I had expected. I would ask if the deadline could be extended to a realistic timeframe. If it can't be extended, I would then ask if there is anyone who can help in order to meeting the deadline."

A poor answer would be: "I would see how much I can get done before the deadline. If I get it finished, then great; if not, I can always finish it tomorrow - it can't be that important."

How would your best friend describe you?

Why: Employers recognize that an inexperienced PA may have had very little work experience on which an employer can judge his or her effectiveness. Asking how a best friend perceives the person is likely to result in an honest response that reveals the candidate's general personality traits. The question may not be posed to a more experienced candidate. This probing question is designed to achieve an open response.

Example of a good answer: "A loyal friend he or she can rely on, who will always listen - and someone who's always willing to try something new." This highlights lots of great attributes for the workplace.

A weak answer would be: "A good friend who's always prepared to have fun." This answer is a missed opportunity to spell out why you are a good friend. The 'fun' element may indicate a party animal who is likely to put her social life first.

How did you measure your success with your last employer?

Why: This question is designed to measure a PA's confidence in his or her achievement in the job. The range of tasks he or she undertakes is likely to be very wide. It forces him or her to identify an important element of the job, and to demonstrate how it was successfully addressed, thereby avoiding any general or vague comments about success. The underlying thought is *'prove how good you are'*.

Example of a good answer: "Let me give you an example" - the answer would then contain hard facts and an example of great results the candidate has achieved. Also, offering to give other examples implies that the list is long.

A poor answer would be: "We don't have any way of measuring success. But I work very hard, and think I do the job very well - and I did get a bonus last year." This answer is far too woolly and subjective, and shows a lack of initiative in failing to come up with a specific example. All of the employer's staff may have received a bonus. It should be made clear if this was on merit.

As the PA to a high-profile individual, you are privy to some sensitive information about your employers personal life – some of it may be not be in tandem with your moral beliefs. How would you deal with this?

Why: The candidate's levels of discretion, sensitivity and understanding of confidentiality, which are vital at this level of PA work, is being measured.

Example of a good answer: "I would get on with my work professionally, keep all information confidential and keep my opinions and judgments to myself."

A weaker answer would be: "I don't like working for certain people."

What did you find to be the most challenging part of your last job?

Why: This measures the level of seniority at which a secretary or PA has worked, by revealing the amount of responsibility in the job. It can also reveal what an individual finds 'challenging', highlight a particular weakness or, more positively, demonstrate how well the individual deals with a tough situation.

Example of a good answer: "Making a presentation to the board on behalf of my boss. I felt very nervous doing this, so I've signed up for a presentation skills course to give me confidence, and to help me give a better presentation next time." This is an excellent answer - making a presentation to the board shows that this PA is obviously high-powered. Her nervousness is understandable. Many people, even high-level executives, find making a presentation daunting. The important point is that he or she has taken positive steps to overcome the difficulty.

A weaker answer would be: "Dealing with high-level clients who complain directly to my boss, who is the chairman. It makes me feel really uncomfortable. I tend to write them a letter, rather than call them back, so it's less confrontational." Learning to deal with complaints effectively is an important part of any PA's role. This example does not demonstrate high-level responsibility, nor does it show any initiative. Some role-play training might help.

Can you give an example of a time when your employer was absent and you were forced to make an important decision? How did you make it? What alternatives did you consider?

Why: The answer to this question will show how independent and confident the prospective employee is. It also shows if he or she is able to make decisions alone, and if he or she takes the most important aspects into consideration. This question highlights a candidate's analytical abilities as well as their ability to work without constant supervision.

Example of a good answer: One that shows the candidate not only has experience of the situation, but that he or she handled it well. For example, "This happened to me once, when my boss went on a mini-vacation, and I discovered that he had not decided on a venue for a very important dinner meeting. I knew a decision had to be made, and that there was no one else who would know enough about the event to decide. I had done a lot of research on locations and costs before he left, so I made a decision on the one I thought would be best, taking all the factors into account."

A weaker answer would be one where the PA defers to the employer: "I believe that the boss should make all major decisions, and for this reason, I do not think it my place to make such a decision on his or her behalf."

How do you feel about working alone for long periods at a time?

Why: The goal is to establish what sort of work environment suits the candidate best and if the candidate knows what it will be like having their employer away for three to four days at a time.

Example of a good answer: "It gives me the opportunity to catch up on any outstanding issues and I enjoy running the home/office in the absence of my employer. Although they may not be present in the office, I would always expect to be called upon while they are traveling, whether it be to rearrange an itinerary, or prepare paperwork."

A poor answer would be: "I don't really like working on my own, as there is no one to talk to, but at least it means I can leave on time."

Dynamics of the Job

An administrative assistant performs clerical assistance to the company or a department as a whole. In contrast, the duties of a **personal assistant** are focused mainly with easing the workload of one particular person.

She needs a general understanding of her employer's career. That is because her basic function is to act as his **'working partner'** or **'complement'** in the performance of those duties and tasks which are involved. She also often has to assist him in decision-making or she is, at the very least, required to obtain or supply information or data upon which he will base his decisions.

An essential aspect of a personal assistant's job, *the importance of which is too often underrated,* is to relieve her employer of many "routine" or "mundane' tasks – in order to leave him freer to concentrate on more important or more pressing career matters. At the same time she needs to be able to "complement" him and to overcome weaknesses or shortcomings he has which could prevent the most successful performance of his duties. To take a simple example, if her employer is weak in spelling, she must ensure that her own spelling is word-perfect so that she can correct any errors he makes. Similarly, if he is forgetful with regard to time, she must ensure that she reminds him of meetings he has to attend or appointments he must keep.

Partnering with your Employer

The ideal working relationship between a PA and her employer is a **'partnership.'** Each 'partner' needs to understand the other – their individual characters, their duties and responsibilities, their skills, talents and abilities, their limitations or shortcomings, and so on, with each attempting *(frequently without conscious thought)* to complement and adapt to the other, to provide an efficient working partnership. Of course, the ideal is one thing, and the reality is very often quite another matter. Unfortunately, it is all too often that the PA, who is expected to do most of the understanding and adapting, is being looked upon as the 'junior' partner.

It is dangerous to categorize the high-profile individual to whom PAs might be assigned or to attempt to create a general description of "a-day-in-the-life." Every single employer will be different, with his own personality or character, temperament, likes and dislikes, preferences and prejudices, talents, skills, abilities, strengths and weaknesses, and so on.

The requirements and expectations of employers from their PAs also vary according to their characters. Some employers are – *or like to think they are* – self reliant and need little, if any, help or advice; often, that is, until their PAs are away or ill or on vacation! There are other employers who are too embarrassed to ask for help; their PAs need to be able to spot quickly when and what help is needed and to take necessary action, often unobtrusively, without being asked. Yet other employers attempt to off-load onto their PAs as much as possible; those PAs must handle this workload with grace. However, a PA must admit when she is overworked and must firmly but tactfully ensure that work and responsibility are sometimes shared between the "partners" if possible.

It can therefore be seen that it is mainly the PA that is expected to "meld" – to merge or to blend in – with her employer(s), rather than the other way around. That is not always easy for her to do for a number of reasons; not the least of which involve her own character, temperament, abilities, and ambitions, etc. However, with patience and tact and understanding, an effective working relationship can generally be formed with even the most "difficult" of employers.

Naturally there are bound to be some failures, as two people with very different characters – or conversely with very similar characters – might not be able to avoid what are called *"personality clashes"*, however hard they might try not to provoke each other. When this occurs, in order to minimize distress, it is best that the partnership is quickly 'dissolved'. The PA concerned must try to find herself a new position and she should not blame herself for the failure as long as she knows that she **did** try her best to make the partnership work.

There are situations in which an assistant may work for multiple employers. Great care and tact are necessary (as well as time management and priority assessment).

Dionne M. Muhammad

Job Descriptions

Just as there is no one "standard" employer and there is no one "standard" PA, there is also no boilerplate job description. Every opportunity to work as a Personal Assistant will be **unique.** That is because not only will the actual work differ, but because the various "characters" involved – *the PA, the celebrity, their colleagues, associates, family and other contacts* – will all differ, and will have some bearing on what is involved in the position and how the work needs to be performed. The differences between each job might be minor or major but they **will** exist.

We will examine a wide range of activities in which PAs **might** be involved; but it is quite impossible for us to state what activities or duties will actually be involved in a specific job. The duties which a particular PA will be expected to perform will vary – perhaps considerably – at different stages during her career. As a PA matures and gains experience and knowledge, she should be able to undertake a greater variety of work and assume greater responsibilities.

The point is that any PA must appreciate her circumstances – her duties can sometimes change at short notice, perhaps with little warning. She needs to be able to adapt to changing circumstances *as* **and** *when* they occur. She must also segue into the altered duties smoothly and efficiently if she is to make a success of her career.

What is looked upon as being **"career success"** might vary from individual to individual. To some people, the measure of success is merely the value of the financial rewards received, while others also seek **"job satisfaction."** The latter seeks an opportunity that will allow them to love their work and to feel worthwhile. Other people seek promotion to more senior positions, not only for the financial rewards and fringe benefits that such advancement brings, but also for the prestige and status. For example, finding a position as an assistant to a producer could lead to that assistant one day actually working as a producer of a major film or television program. An assistant at a talent agency may one day wind up as an agent, representing celebrities. Yet other people strive to secure promotion because they enjoy accepting greater responsibility, or even revel in authority and in managing others, or because they must simply satisfy some inner urge to "get ahead."

There are increasing numbers of people too, who today see successful careers in PA positions as being satisfactory enough for them. These people enjoy working as part of "Team Hollywood" and have chosen **"assisting"** as their career of choice. The very fact that you have embarked on a quest to learn more about the role of a Personal Assistant, shows that you are intent on making a success of your career in this field, by whatever terms you might gauge that success. Therefore, it is necessary for us to look now at some of the personal "attributes" which you will need to possess or to develop if you are to have the best chances of achieving success.

Desirable Traits:

- Time management skills

- Articulate

- Good judgment

- Tactful, diplomatic, pleasant

- Excellent memory

- Security minded

- Knowledge of emergency procedures

- Quick thinker

- Knowledge of the industry and key players in your
  employer's field of discipline

- Flexibility and adaptability

- Non-judgmental

- Ability to anticipate whims

- Project planning and management skills

- Computer basics and internet savvy

- Administrative skills

- Ability to take dictation or fast notes

- Resourcefulness, ability to utilize multiple sources
  to find information

A Day in the Life

Being a personal assistant sounds like a glamorous job doesn't it? In some cases it is a glamorous job that allows for you to become exposed to some of the accoutrements that come with being successful and rich. But in most cases, your day to day tasks will be far removed from the red-carpet. We followed the personal assistant to an award winning musician for a day. The assistant also supports her boss's wife, who is the founder of an advertising agency

7.15 am

PA arrives at the home office early. Boss is up and already on the phone. He is on the phone for a 7.30am meeting to discuss an overseas tour but the daycare doesn't open until just before nine and the nanny has called in sick. The PA entertains the toddler, giving her breakfast and organizing her lunch, before driving her to the day care *(the wife is out of town on a business trip)*.

9.00 am

Back at the office, PA contacts the caterer to do lunch for an afternoon meeting the Boss is having off-site. Now that the Boss is out of his morning conference call, PA clears the catering choices with him that she has selected for the lunch meeting.

9.20 am

Boss has written his usual brief of things PA is to do:

- Find the name of the producer for a video the Boss saw on television last night.

- Locate last week's New York Times

- Find a publisher willing to donate $5000 worth of books as a prize for the Boss's charity - Reading Camp for Kids

- Purchase an inflatable beach ball and foot pump for the wife to take with her on an upcoming trip to Maui

- Buy 150 plastic brochure holders (wall mounting) for the wife's newly launched advertising agency

- Develop a list of 6 key attractions/things to do in Maui as well as things to do in Auckland for upcoming visits

- Find out prices for children's tickets to both Maui and Auckland

- Find a credible nanny to be available for the upcoming trips just in case the family's nanny has not recovered and is unable to make the trip(s).

And:

- Get product merchandise from a retailer

- Organize a driver to meet the wife's clients at the airport

- get new battery for Boss's watch

- Get money out of account to pay childcare

- Sort the mail

- Get a courier to retrieve a video of the latest episode of 'Friends'

- Organize flowers for a client

12.45 pm

The PA is well into the list by now, having gotten through at least a third. But it is lunch time now, and like anyone – she has to eat! She notices that the Boss won't have time to grab anything as he has been in non stop meetings since 10. The PA drives and picks up the Boss's favorite lunch and drink, deposits it on his desk with napkins and utensils, and retires to the kitchen for a break.

1.45 pm

Boss leaves the office for a meeting, PA returns to her list.

2.00 pm

Wife calls in from her business trip and asks PA to meet with her graphic designer to offer a fresh perspective for project. PA puts down what she is doing, makes coffee and awaits the arrival of the graphic designer. Graphic designer arrives, PA conferences the wife in and suggests a few ideas. Once the wife is satisfied – the PA is back on track, she returns to her list.

3.30 pm

PA heads to the location of the off-site meeting. She places the agenda on the seats of the attendees. The caterer arrives to deliver the food - PA sets up tea and coffee and then returns to her list in an adjoining room while the meeting is going on.

4.00 pm

Boss is running late for the meeting. As the attendees arrive, the PA takes them to the meeting room and offers, then serves them all something to drink. She apologizes for the Boss's tardiness. She keeps them entertained until the Boss arrives at 4.10 pm.

4.30 pm

The daycare calls, the toddler has become very upset and his head is warm. The PA drives over to the center to retrieve the baby; she drops off the Boss's dry-cleaning and takes a trip to the post-office along the way.

5.00 pm

PA returns to the house, checks the toddler's temperature and once she discovers that it is normal, she calls the emergency babysitter. While she is awaiting the babysitter's arrival, she entertains the toddler while still attending to her list, answering the phone, taking messages, making orders and planning the Boss's meetings for tomorrow. Once the babysitter arrives she prepares to return to the meeting site.

5.05 pm

Before she can leave the house, UPS delivers some products for a sampling campaign the wife's agency is running. PA unpacks the product, arranges it into piles and packs it into bags for distribution.

6.00 pm

PA heads back to the meeting site. She arrives a few minutes before they adjourn. Once they are done, she thanks the attendees for coming and ensures that their parking is validated. She also requests the business cards of the individuals that she is unfamiliar with. Next, she assists the caterer with cleaning and organizing the room back to normal. She asks her Boss whether he needs anything.

7.15 pm

PA returns back to the house. Before leaving for the day, she goes over the to-do list with the Boss. They add new things and re-prioritize items that are in progress.

8:00 – until **(SHE IS ON CALL)**

Whew! What is her secret? "You basically need to be flexible and think ahead." For every situation, she pondered: *What does this mean for my boss(es)? What will they need done today?*

If you want to be a successful personal assistant, you must have the following qualities:
- patience
- creativity and lateral thinking
- an excellent phone manner
- exemplary computer and typing skills
- ability to multi task and work deadlines due yesterday
- a good work ethic with attention to detail
- a bit of psychic ability to think what boss requires

Interview Cheat Sheet

This is a document you prepare before important meetings. It is a personal briefing to you, from you. It helps you remember key facts, such as your major accomplishments, and serious questions or concerns. You don't read from the sheet, but you do keep it handy, and if convenient, you may want to review it as your interview is ending to be certain you didn't forget anything critical.

Day and Date:

Meeting With:

Name

Title

Company

    City, State Zip

    Telephone

    FAX

    Mobile/Pager

    E-mail

Major Accomplishments:

    1.

    2.

    3.

    4.

Management or Work Style:

    1.

    2.

    3.

    4.

Things You Need to Know About Me:

    1.

    2.

    3.

    4.

Reasons I Left Last Job:

    1.

    2.

    3.

    4.

Answers to Difficult Questions:

    1.

    2.

    3.

    4.

My Strengths/Weaknesses:

    1.

    2.

    3.

    4.

Questions to Ask Interviewer:

    1.

    2.

    3.

    4.

Dionne M. Muhammad

Things I Can Do For You:

1.

2.

3.

4.

What I Wore (*to prevent wearing the same clothing repeatedly*):

Characteristics Needed for Success

Personal Assistants act as the key liaison in the lives of their high-profile employers. From greeting clients and associates to attending meetings in an employer's stead; the way PAs portray themselves in terms of appearance, communication and etiquette is extremely important. Not every desirable "attribute" that we will describe in the following section will apply to every person who holds, or intends to hold, a PA position. However, all of these should be kept in mind as many of these characteristics will be looked for during the interview process for a personal assistant position.

Appearance

It is important for a Personal Assistant to present an attractive and pleasing appearance so she creates a good impression on all with whom she comes into contact with during the course of her duties. An assistant might be the first person with whom a visitor speaks with on the phone or comes into contact with at the celebrity's home or an executive's office. If she creates a good impression, that will reflect favorably on her employer and even on the enterprise.

By "attractive" we do not mean "beauty", contrary to popular belief. Most celebrities do not seek "sexily" or "flashily/scantily attired assistants." Most prefer an assistant that is always neatly and tastefully dressed. No matter who you assist, you should keep in mind that your role is to operate as *someone* that provides lifestyle and business support and you must at all times reflect a business-person.

A PA whose duties include dealing with the associates, clients, friends, agents, managers, etc., of the celebrity will usually be expected to dress in a manner which will enhance the image which her employer wishes to convey; modern, conservative, dignified, efficient, unruffled, and so on, as appropriate. On the other hand, PAs who have little if any contact with "external" associates and contacts might be permitted to wear somewhat more casual clothes, with in reason. Whatever is worn, must however, always be clean, neat and tidy and well pressed. A PA's hair must be clean and well-groomed at all times and she should avoid extremes of fashion.

Reminder: *You are **NOT** the celebrity – you are on the "business" side of "show-business." It is not important for you to wear the latest, trendy, attention getting clothes. You should try to find the balance between fashionable and conservative.*

Personal Assistants should also pay attention to her fingernails; dirty or badly bitten finger nails are not attractive. Likewise, extremely long nails can interfere with typing and with efficient operation of other equipment such as computer keyboards. Particular attention must also be paid to personal hygiene at all times.

> *Note: We are referring to Personal Assistants as **she** throughout the book, only as a matter of convenience. However, please be aware that the information contained in these pages applies to men as well. In the area of grooming; neat and tidy appearances are important for men. Suitable apparel for male assistants might include neckties, sport jackets and blazers. Males must also pay special attention to the grooming of hair and to shaving or to the grooming of any facial hair worn.*

Personality

A pleasing personality is usually most important, as **every** PA will need to maintain good and amicable relations with many different people, in addition to her immediate employer. Most Personal Assistants in the entertainment industry work for one person. However, there are others who work at management companies or talent agencies and they not only serve the manager to which they are assigned, but often assist the clients (i.e. celebrities) with their needs. They may also have significant contact with the "assistants" of other celebrities.

In addition, an assistant, during the course of her duties, will come in contact with existing associates of the celebrity they assist. This includes, but is not limited to: attorneys, accountants, managers, and others with whom the celebrity deals. The ability to get along well with a wide variety of people and to be able to mix easily with them is especially important.

Personality is not something which is easy to define but is made up of very many different and individual characteristics, personal traits and mannerisms. Different PA jobs might call for people with different personalities. Some are most suitable for those with bright, cheerful, outgoing personalities; while others call for people with cool, calm, collected and even stern personalities, to give just two contrasting examples.

Common personality traits required; however, will include amiability, the willingness to be helpful to others, patience, tact and politeness; which together ensure a pleasant, even temper and self control. (*...especially necessary during particularly busy or rush periods like during album releases and tours, awards ceremonies or filming of movies or football season*). The foregoing are important, as nobody likes to have to work with a bad tempered, excitable person!

PROFILE: 29 year old single male

RESIDENCE: Beverly Hills (living with employer)

EMPLOYER: Producer

"There are going to be times that you are given a set of tasks to complete and when you do … you may hear from your boss 'That is not what I asked you to do!' ….. Don't be surprised to hear "That is not what I said,' or 'Weren't you listening?" When I started my current job 2 years ago, my boss would often give me vague instructions like "Call Tom and tell him to meet me at the usual place around 10am ….." he would then walk away. I would just sit there in disbelief. I remember asking myself *"Does he really think I'm his old assistant – who the hell is Tom?"* I followed him to his office and said, "excuse me but who is Tom?" He soon realized that he hadn't provided me with the information I needed to get the task done. When you start a new position, you must sit with the boss and get the information you need to empower you to do the job well. If you are in situations where you are given instructions, write them down —- and then read them back to your boss to make sure you are on the same page ….. That way, you may hear less expressions like *"That is not what I told you to do."* And even if you hear it …. You have a record of what was actually said. You should never use your documented record to dispute with the employer …. but just for your own peace of mind, so that you will know that you aren't crazy and can hear clearly.

Communication

Instructions and other types of **information will flow** "down" to the personal assistant from her employer and at the same time and —- just as importantly —— a summary of results and other information flows "up" to the employer from the assistant. In other words, there should be a **two way flow of information** – both "downwards" as well as "upwards". Assistants to most celebrities will be concerned both with imputing relevant information into the two-way flow, and receiving or extracting required information from the two-way flow.

Memoranda

In many cases, the PA and her employer can communicate with each other quickly and conveniently orally – by word of mouth – in face to face conversations, by telephone or by email. However, there are other instances, e.g. when figures or amounts have to be recorded or meetings have to be arranged, when it is advisable to put communications "in writing". That might be done manually or by typing and the message might be sent internally "by hand" to the addressee (s) or by fax or by email. Such an internal written communication – by whichever method it is transmitted – is called a 'memorandum' (abbreviation 'memo'); the plural is 'memoranda' (abbreviation 'memos')

The employer might write out a memo himself by hand. It is advisable for the PA to purchase "pads" of carbon-backed blank paper for the employer to write the memo so there will be a copy of the original information that was recorded. More generally, he will dictate the text of the memo to his

PA or give her notes from which she will produce it. She too should use the carbon pad and after taking the notes, provide the employer with the original and then carry out the instructions using the information on the copy.

It is advantageous to use a memo to convey a message which contains figures (amounts, dates, times, values, etc.) or some other information which could be misunderstood, misinterpreted or forgotten if simply given orally. Frequently a memo is produced as a "follow-up" to an oral conversation (whether face to face or by telephone) to confirm what was said or what was decided during it. Because copies of memos are retained on file, there is always a written record of the messages conveyed; which generally there is not when messages are passed orally alone.

***Status Reports:** Assistants should periodically create a report that records the tasks they have performed. When assisting a celebrity with their complex lifestyle and business needs it may be impossible to chronicle every task. However, if you can document your activities daily, that would be a plus. At the end of the month, present your employer with a status report which outlines everything that you have completed on their behalf, as well as the outstanding issues and ongoing tasks that are still in progress. It is not necessary to be redundant in the report by listing every day the tasks that are routine in nature, such as "I opened the mail," I checked your voice messages…"*

Adaptability

During the course of her career a PA is likely to hold a number of positions with various employers which can require her to perform widely different tasks; as each will have a different character and different requirements. For the assistant who is 'blessed' to work for the same employer for many years, changes will also occur as the celebrity's career grows, slows down, grows again, becomes erratic...... A successful PA will be able to **adapt** quickly and smoothly to the changed circumstances so that her efficiency is unimpaired. In cases where an assistant goes to work for a new employer, she might have to adapt her whole approach in order to "meld" effectively with their character, temperament and lifestyle needs. She might even have to adapt or modify her personality, as outwardly displayed to others, to fit into the new environment. For example, an assistant who works with a United States Congressman, may be expected to demonstrate a more moderate, dignified and responsible attitude than might have been previously necessary as a PA on tour with a musician. Adaptability or flexibility of mind also applies on a smaller, but no less important, scale for day to day work; as a PA must be prepared and able to leave off performing one task and switch quickly and smoothly to performing another. Quite often she might have to abruptly stop what she is doing and start on other work which her employer considers urgent (or work which circumstances dictate has become urgent) or which he wants done "at once". She also needs the ability to decide – correctly – on the order of priority in which more routine work will be performed, so that all is completed satisfactorily and on time.

PROFILE: 35 year old mother of a 9 yr old daughter

RESIDENCE: Marina Del Rey, California

EMPLOYER: Well known television actress

"I started working for [the actress] after spending 6 years with my previous employer and it was a welcome change. I used to work for a financial advisor and private accountant that had a lot of celebrity clients. However, my day to day activities were so predictable. I really needed a change. The flexibility that I enjoyed when I worked for the actress was wonderful the first few months. **And then it happened.** The rush period was upon us. She had 3 projects going on at once. I had to manage her calendar, schedule her appointments, and work with her publicist and agent on appearances and interviews. I was taking care of her, her house, her business, her family. **It was crazy!** I thought I was going to lose my mind. I went from a regular shift of 8-4 to being on call 24/7. Before I went to work for her – I knew there would be times that we would be busy … but I never expected it to be this intense. It was like being in labor —– the mental pain was sometimes unbearable. I have been with her for 2 years now and have learned how to prepare myself for it. I exercise regularly, do yoga and meditation and I have to eat right. I also spend lots of time with my daughter when times are slow, because during the more intense season – I may have to travel frequently. All in all, it has been an interesting experience."

Mental Agility

A good PA needs to be mentally **alert** and **attentive**, needs to be able to think clearly, to be receptive to new ideas, to grasp quickly and to react quickly to new instructions and changed circumstances (that is adaptability). She needs to be able to **reason** and to **analyze,** to possess **imagination**, and to display **initiative**; it is important that she does not have to be told how to perform every little task, even if it is slightly out of the ordinary.

Quite often – due either to the absence of her employer or because he is otherwise occupied – a PA will have to use her **initiative** and make decisions on her own. Such decisions as those should be based on her knowledge of the work performed by her employer and on her experience of what he would likely do or want her to do in similar circumstances. At the earliest opportunity she should inform the celebrity of the decision she made or the action she initiated and her reasons for doing so

- to keep him fully "in the picture" and aware of the situation

And

- to give him the opportunity to make any modifications if necessary

In order for her to be able to use her initiative to make decisions and to initiate action, a PA needs **confidence** in herself. She also must be confident in her personal knowledge and abilities. Such self-confidence comes with experience and maturity. It is important; however, that such confidence does not lead to conceit or to arrogance which can easily offend others or to "overconfidence" which can all too easily result in mistakes and accidents. The more senior the PA position – the more mature are the mental ability and sense of responsibility that needs to be displayed.

Your Health

A celebrity needs a PA who will be able to work well, consistently, one who will not be "away" often because of "ill health" or whose performance will frequently be adversely affected by illness (or by some other "personal problems"). It might seem unfair to penalize a person for health issues over which she might not have control, but on the other hand, an employer will be penalized, and his work will suffer if he does not have the continuous support and backing of his Personal Assistant. (At the same time), a PA needs the ability to "hold the fort" during periods in which her employer is ill or is away for other business or personal reasons.

A PA needs to be able to **see well** in order to read documents, contracts, computer screens, and so on, depending on the work to be performed. If necessary, glasses or contact lenses should be worn. **Good hearing** is also an important physical attribute for a PA especially for telephone work, taking instructions from the employer and for taking dictation if needed.

In many cases, particularly during "rush" periods, **stamina** is required to enable a PA to work long and hard without undue stress or strain. Physical fitness contributes to mental fitness or alertness, which as we have already seen, is so important for a Personal Assistant.

"I was so baffled when I called a well-known music producer's studio and his assistant answered the phone. She spoke so much slang. I expected her to present a more professional demeanor since after all; this was a place of business that I was contacting."

- A.R., Entertainment Industry Publicist.

Speaking Well

A respected Personal Assistant has **good diction**. That is the ability to speak clearly, in a pleasant, well modulated and efficient sounding voice. She needs a **wide vocabulary**, by which we mean she must have knowledge of and the ability to spell and use correctly a wide variety of words. She needs the ability **to express herself clearly** and **fluently** without resorting to "slang" terms and expressions or to frequent crutches like "ums" and "ahs." **Good** and **clear speech** is particularly important when using the telephone and when receiving or dealing with visitors, so that callers gain a good impression of the speaker and of the employing celebrity.

Some PA's may have to write letters and other correspondence on behalf of their employer. PAs may also have to supervise household or office staff, which again requires them to speak well and clearly. In addition more and more employers are requiring their assistants to be bilingual.

In addition to speaking well, a PA needs to be able to **write well.** Her **punctuation** must also be good, as frequently those dictating do not indicate where commas and other punctuation marks are to be placed: thus she must herself decide, correctly where to place them. Further, proper grammar is key. Her **spelling,** too must be excellent because –

- the person dictating may use words which they might be uncertain how to spell;

And

- because, as mentioned earlier, you may work with an employer who is weak in spelling and they rely on their PAs to correct their spelling errors.

A good written and typed, attractively laid-out and neat business letter gives a good impression of its writer and the employer on whose behalf it was written. Another reason for needing good command of the language(s) used is that a PA might often have to check, and if necessary correct and improve, the work of the celebrity they work for or of others subordinate to them. She may also have to teach the other household or business staffs how to write and or type letters and other documents to an acceptable standard.

Accuracy

Most, if not all, of the many different tasks performed by PA's require attention to detail and accuracy. Carelessness, lack of attention or concentration, inaccuracies, etc, by a PA can easily lead to mistakes, delays, misunderstandings, complaints, and even to loss of money or opportunities that are part of the celebrity's job. They can cause problems for the employer who will quickly lose confidence in the assistant.

Even seemingly "minor" errors, such as the misfiling of a document, can cause problems, and can waste much time and effort in locating and correcting the mistakes. The need for accuracy and care extends to the completion of forms and other business documents to the making of accounting entries into the household ledger, and other records (manual or computerized), to maintaining a filing system, and to many other tasks such as scheduling appointments, travel arrangements, keeping a contact database, etc.

Some PAs might be require to handle the checkbook and to control and record petty cash expenditures. This requires strict **accuracy** and attention **to detail.** A simple mistake could lead your employer to the conclusion that you have misused their funds. In most cases, employers provide the assistant with a credit card and a separate checking account which may limit their exposure to a substantial amount of money. In any event, it is important to keep up with receipts and to log all expenses in the appropriate category so that your employer or their accountant can reconcile the books.

Clear, neat **handwriting** is an important feature in accuracy, as an unclear or badly written word can lead to miscalculation, misunderstanding or misinterpretation, all of which can cause possibly serious problems at the very least, time and work will be wasted in tracing and correcting errors. A PA needs an **orderly** mental attitude toward her work – from which care and accuracy will result. Outward evidence of such a state of mind will be a neat and tidy desk and general work area – which might be a "private office" – shelves, filing systems, etc. The ability to **concentrate** without being easily distracted is also important.

PROFILE: 27 year old single female

RESIDENCE: New York, New York

EMPLOYER: Works for couple (Film Producer and Author)

"My bosses, particularly the wife who is a writer, do not like to be disturbed that often during the business day. I have a list of people that I can put through when they call the office; but mainly they want their calls screened. **I am the official gatekeeper**. I have worked for them for 3 years, but when I first started I have a funny story to share ... the cell phone that they gave me to use was also used by their former assistant. Everybody in their life has that number. A gentleman (let's call him Paul) called the office and asked to speak with the husband/film producer. I informed Paul that he was extremely busy and did not want to be disturbed (that was the instructions I was given earlier that day). Paul yelled at me ... **called me the "B" word** and demanded that I put (the former assistant) on the phone. I explained to him that I was the family's new assistant and was instructed NOT to put any calls through. He hung up on me. He then called the cell phone .. and guess who answered? He went on to give me his resume — telling me how long he has known the family ... how he does business with the husband all the time — and how instructions to 'not put calls through' **do not apply to him.** Nevertheless, I did **NOT** put Paul through. Well, as it turns out, Paul was right! Those instructions did not apply to him. He still shouldn't have called me a "B" (he later apologized). And I learned that when an employer tells you that they are not taking calls ... you must always ask them *"Are there any exceptions?"* Just in case your boss has a Paul in his life.

Telephone Courtesy

Screening phone calls is a delicate and tricky business. When callers are asked their name, put on hold, and then told that the person they are calling is unavailable, they are quite likely to take this response personally. As a "professional" Personal Assistant, you need clear direction from your employer on how to handle callers. It is in everyone's best interest to manage screening with tact. The way the caller is treated will determine future business and personal relationships.

If an employer does not want to take any calls without a screen, the most courteous way to do this is to tell the unidentified caller that the other person is in a meeting, out of the office or is on the phone before asking who is calling. Then offer to take a message and have the call returned.

If the caller is someone who should be connected, the assistant can announce that "Mr. X" suddenly has become available. After a while people will catch on that this employer is hiding behind his assistant and is inaccessible to callers. If this is your practice, you might want to rethink it, depending on the image that you want to portray. Busy people can't take all calls, but the other extreme of not taking *any* may not be the best business decision.

If your job is to screen calls, use the most polite questions. There are a number of choices. You can use traditional screens that begin with "May I," such as "May I tell Mr. X who is calling?" or "May I have your number?" An indirect screen begins with "Let me," for instance, "Let me tell her the name of your company." And then there is the fill-in-the-blank query: "And your call is regarding …?" or "And you are with …?"

Never ask simply, "Who's calling?" Such a direct question is abrupt and insensitive. Other curt questions to avoid are "What do you do?" and "Does he know who you are?"

---

*When you are the **caller**, there is a very simple way to avoid this screening altogether. Whenever you place a call, identify yourself by name and company and say why you are calling before asking to speak to anyone. You will avoid putting yourself and others in an awkward situation.*

You should try to make every caller feel important by being friendly, polite and professional on the phone. Use the following techniques to leave a good impression with each caller.

- Keep an updated list of individuals your employer wants to speak with no-matter-what – this will often be their spouse, agent, attorney or other extremely relevant people in their life. You should be careful about playing "gatekeeper" to these type of individuals unless you are specifically asked to do so.
- Smile when you talk. A smile helps you sound more relaxed and pleasant.
- Speak clearly into the receiver. Avoid slang or technical terms.

- Use proper grammar and diction. Avoid "yep," "uh-huh" and "OK." Instead use "yes," "certainly" or "absolutely."

- Answer the phone within three rings. A phone that rings more than three times gives a caller the impression that you don't want to take the call.

- Always tell the caller your name.

- Give the caller a friendly greeting, such as "Good morning" or "Good evening," and ask how you may help him or her.

- Give the caller your complete attention. Pretend he or she is standing in front of you.

- Talk only to the person on the phone, not to anyone else around you.

- If the call is for your employer, ask the caller if you may put him or her on hold. Then get the employer immediately or take a message if necessary.

- To take a message, write down the caller's name, the time and date of the call, the message and your name as the message taker, just in case there are any questions.

You will often be very busy when the phone rings. To make callers feel welcome, catch your breath before picking up the phone. If you sound stressed or hurried, the caller will also feel rushed. Sometimes, to take care of a request you will need to put a caller on hold. **Providing good service means always asking callers if it is all right to put them on hold.** If a caller gives you permission, take care of the request quickly. Thank the caller for waiting when you return to the line. Always end each phone call with a sincere, "Thank you for calling." Offer to be of assistance in the future, and let the caller hang up first. The end of your call is your last chance to leave a good impression with your employer's associates.

"Dependability is a 'gold standard' which transforms an intelligent, thoughtful, and proficient PA from merely good to truly exceptional. A dependable PA is one an employer can rely on without as much as a second thought. You're there when you need to be, frequently before. You not only double, but triple check every detail. And you pride yourself on the fact that this standard not only reflects well on you, but unerringly places your employer in the best light possible. The gold standard of dependability is the basic foundation for trust, respect and professional success."

– **Janice Naehu** (former Personal Assistant of eight years) to David Koepp – screenwriter, Spider-Man, Hack, Panic Room, Stir of Echoes, Jurassic Park, Carlito's Way, Toy Soldiers, Death Becomes Her ….

Sense of Responsibility

A celebrity needs to be able to **rely** on his PA; to **depend** upon her to provide the support and backup he needs in the efficient performance of his work. He must be able to **trust** her to work well and thoroughly without constant supervision, throughout the day – to arrive at work on time and not to leave early, day after day – and to complete her "share" of the work. He must also be able to rely upon her to "deputize" for him when the necessity arises and to rely on her to use her initiative in dealing with matters that arise which, for one reason or another, he cannot immediately deal with himself.

In other words, a celebrity wants – and needs – a PA who is **reliable, dependable** and **trustworthy.**

She must also be **honest.** That extends not only to the safekeeping of valuables entrusted to her, such as money, petty cash, blank checks, stationary, signature stamps, etc; but also to maintaining **confidentiality.** Quite often during the course of her duties, a PA might be entrusted with confidential information; that is facts, figures and documents not intended to be generally known, it is essential that she keeps confidential all such information as it comes into her possession.

She must resist any attempts by others to obtain from her confidential information which she has not been authorized to communicate to them. The various attributes which we have mentioned such as reliability, dependability, trustworthiness, honesty and integrity all combine to form what is called a **'sense of responsibility.'** The possession of such a sense of responsibility is essential for progress. It encompasses many facets, in addition to those already mentioned:

- care to prevent damage to or losses of any assets (possessions) of the employer;
- action to secure and to retain positive relationships with their associates

And

- care for others in preventing accidents and inquiry to colleagues and visitors alike.

I do everything that I can to improve my skills. I take computer classes, learn event management … I want to make myself indispensable to my boss

- N.H. Los Angeles based assistant.

Self Improvement

This book contains many of the personal attributes that can be deemed as traits of the most successful personal assistants. Of course, not everybody can be expected to have them all, but many of these skills **can,** if not already possessed, be acquired and/or developed. Every person aspiring to be a successful Celebrity Personal Assistant should first take a good, long, hard – and honest – look at herself, and decide which of the attributes we have described she currently lacks.

Having decided that, the second step should be to make a determined attempt to remedy the situation. That might not really be quite as difficult as it might seem, for example:

- If her sense of dress is not good, she should seek advice from someone with an "eye" to what suits her best.

- Similarly, if necessary, she can obtain professional advice on what hair style, make-up, etc, suits her best.

- If she is shy, she must make a conscious effort to meet and to mix with other people.

- If she is emotional or quick tempered, she must make a sustained effort to keep calm and collected – and to keep a hold over her temper whatever the provocation.

- If her spelling is weak, she should obtain a good dictionary and refer to it whenever necessary.

- If her math skills are weak, she should make use of a pocket calculator, and train herself to cross check all calculations she makes.

- If her vocabulary is not vast, purchase a thesaurus and a book of worn-out-words and phrases as a means of expanding the number of word she knows and uses when communicating.

Many similar examples can be given, and it is important that action **is taken** to remedy any recognized shortcomings. The greater the efforts made, the greater will be the chances of a person making a success in her chosen profession – and it should never be forgotten that Personal Assisting **is** a profession.

Etiquette Tips

Etiquette is a land with no visible borders. A warm *"Hello, how are you? How may I be of assistance?"* may be among the standard greetings from a personal assistant to those she comes in contact with via telephone or in person.

PA's should become very familiar with using the appropriate greetings and phrases. Her familiarity with protocol reaches beyond the borders of the United States since most A-list celebrities have international reach.

A well-trained PA is above making wrong turns on the road to etiquette. She knows that the distance she has to maintain with a Mexican guest differs from that with an English one. And if there's anyone qualified to set up warning signboards at a dinner party, it has to be her.

As a PA, you have to know what to say, what not to say, when to smile, how much eye contact to make, and above all, be sincere in every gesture you make. What you say has to match your actions.

- Don't criticize or trash your employers' competition to anyone. What you don't say can make a powerful statement about your personal dignity.
- Do leave your bad mood at the door and don't take out your anger on others.
- Don't gossip and don't listen to gossip.
- Do converse with the persons seated on each side of you. One or both of them may be "charm free." This does not mean you should be.
- Do write thank-you notes and letters after receiving a special favor from someone.

- Don't pick your teeth at the table, either with a toothpick or with your fingers. If something gets caught in your teeth, excuse yourself and take care of the problem in the privacy of the restroom.

- Don't place a handbag of any size on a desk, boardroom table, or restaurant table. Small handbags are kept on the lap; larger ones by the side of your chair or near the feet.

- Don't begin eating until everyone has been served when you are seated with a small group. When seated at a long banquet table, you may begin eating after those in your immediate area (about eight persons) have been served.

- Do be prepared for toasting at dinners in restaurants or homes. You must participate or you will be considered socially unsophisticated. However, international protocol dictates that you do not toast a guest of higher rank, one who is older than you are, or the host or hostess, unless he or she initiates the toast.

- Do leave your plate where it is when you have finished eating, with the knife and fork in the 10:20 o'clock position. Place the tips of the utensils at 10 and the handles at 4.

- Don't mind criticism. If it is untrue, disregard it. If it is unfair, keep from irritation. If it is ignorant, smile. If it is justified, learn from it.

World Class Dining

"Eating is not an executive skill...but it is especially hard to imagine why anyone negotiating a rise to the top would consider it possible to skip mastering the very simple requirements...what else did they skip learning?"

Yes, we're all judged by our table manners and we judge others by their table manners. Follow these tips to be at ease as a guest or host/hostess and you'll be judged favorably. *Bon appétit.*

1. **Taking your seat at the table.** Move to the right of your chair and enter from your left side. Exit the same way.

2. **Resist the urge to touch anything on the table.** Your elbows or forearms are never placed on the table. Continental style, wrists may rest on the table. American style, one wrist rests on the table and the other on the lap, or both rest on the lap.

3. **The host leads the way.** Wait for the host to pick up his or her napkin before picking up yours. If there is no host, wait until at least three people are seated. Do not unfold the napkin until it is on your lap. Place your napkin on the chair when excusing yourself.

4. **Wait for the host to start eating.** The host signals the beginning of each course.

5. **BMW.** Your bread place is on your left, your meal is in the center, and your water is on your right. Knives and spoons are on your right; forks are on your left.

6. **Soup is spooned away from you**. Sip the soup from the side of the spoon. Place the spoon on the under plate when you are resting and when you have finished.

7. **Keep your elbows close to your sides.** Bring the food to your face, not your face to your food.

8. **Taste your food before salting**. Pass from hand to table and do not use them first.

9. **When you finish a course, place your knife and fork in the 10:20 o'clock position.** American style: tines up. Continental style: tines down.

10. **The host signifies the end of the meal by placing his/her napkin on the table.** Place your unfolded napkin on the left side of your plate or in the center if your plate has been removed.

Time Management

When you are responsible for the success of someone else by playing an important role on their support team; it is imperative that you direct your time wisely in order to manage their lifestyle – but also to keep your own life balanced. It's not enough to rely on flying by the seat of your pants; a Personal Assistant must keep their work under control by organizing themselves and their time.

Organizing Yourself to Expand the Time Available

No **Personal Assistant** ever has enough time. The problem; however, is not a lack of that inelastic resource, but rather, a matter of how it is used. Time is an unforgiving measure of PA's effectiveness therefore time management is key to the success. As a PA you are faced with three annoying questions:

> *How fast can you do it?*
> *How long will it take?*
> *Will it be done on time?*

Time management is really about managing yourself and your energy. In order to manage your time, you must first get an accurate picture of how you are actually using your time by keeping a daily log of your activities. Daily activities should be divided into 3 categories: **Routine work**, **Regular work**, and **Special-project work**.

Routine Work involves tasks that can be done when you have time. These are low-priority items that should take no more than 30 percent of your workday or workweek.

An example of routine tasks can be things such as opening and sorting mail; checking the voice messages in the morning and making a log of the calls for your employer.

Regular Work involves the important tasks that are the heart and soul of your job. These items should take up to 50 to 60 percent of your time.

As a PA to a high-profile person, your "Regular Work" may fluctuate daily. It depends on the project your employer is currently working on. For example, if you are working for a musician who is currently recording an album – your tasks could be scheduling studio time and ensuring all of the activities needed to complete the recording & publishing of the album are done on time.

Special-project work involves high-priority but infrequent tasks that take your attention completely away from your regular work. Special project work probably takes up to 10 to 20 percent of your time. Often special project tasks have no recommended approach, so you will have to find it.

Maximizing Your Time

It is critical to clarify your objectives and determine your priorities every day. Time is your most important resource so every action you take represents a priority decision, whether made consciously or unconsciously. The problem is never that you can't do something; there isn't anything the employer gives you that you can't do. The problem is time, eventually you run out of it.

The first thing you want to do is establish some overall strategy around which you can plan your daily work priorities. The sensible thing is to start each day by meeting briefly with your employer. Based on their order of importance, set your priorities according to their due dates and/or importance of various tasks.

Working in Harmony

Everyone has a "personal style" on how they handle their assigned responsibilities. Career success depends on how well you are able to get cooperation from key people. An effective way of doing this is to show them that your style is very much like theirs. When people interact with others whose personal style is similar to theirs, they seem to be more comfortable. It then becomes easier to gain agreement, cooperation, and understanding from them.

The first step to maximizing your professional relationships is to identify your employer's personal style. This can be identified by a person's speech, dress, and body language. Your success might well depend on how well you "harmonize" with a diverse group of people.

Communicating Effectively with Difficult People

When we do not respond appropriately to someone, communication may become strained and unpleasant. You must demonstrate respect for difficult people by tolerating their behavior with understanding. Sometimes it may be you who, because of an inappropriate remark, takes an otherwise neutral situation and turns it into a difficult one. Such a situation may occur because the other person did not communicate clearly and you did not take the time to clarify his or her meaning before jumping in or you did not use good listening skills.

Communicating effectively is really about listening. There are several tools you can use to show someone that you recognize and accept his or her context:

- You can repeat, or parrot, the person's exact words in a question.
- You can paraphrase the person's message by restating it – in your own words – and asking confirmation, or
- You can reflect the feelings that the person's words or body language conveyed to you.

When dealing with a difficult person you should use empathetic listening. This shows the other person that you value them, even though at the moment they may sound unreasonable. An empathetic response is designed for use when the difficult person is communicating emotionally. It is important to let difficult people know you have heard what they said and move them from their emotional state into a problem-solving frame of mind. An empathetic response has three distinct parts:

- After the difficult person makes a comment, respond with a comment that sounds both supportive and sympathetic.
- Provide a brief explanation that addresses the person's concern.
- Finish with an open-ended question.

When communicating, use the following techniques to help avoid communication barriers:

- Prepare what you are going to say.
- Organize your thoughts, be brief and sequence the topics.

- Arrange for a specific time and place to communicate; make an appointment.
- Tell the person how long the conversation will take.
- Communicate one item at a time.
- Make good eye contact.
- During your conversation, validate continuously with questions.
- Speak the person's name.

Dealing with difficult personalities is an unfortunate reality but becoming aware of another person's communication style can save you from falling into unpleasant exchanges.

Speaking with Confidence and Diplomacy

In order to achieve results when working for a high profile individual (or for anyone for that matter), a PA must be strong and direct. Yet at times this is difficult to do and setting boundaries is even harder. Therefore, assertion is necessary to achieve results. Assertion is an active, rather than passive, approach to life. It involves communication that is open, direct, honest, and appropriate. The purpose of assertiveness is to enable you to act in your own best interests, to stand up for yourself without undue anxiety, to express honest feelings comfortably, and to exercise your own rights without denying the rights of others. An assertive response is one that endeavors to accomplish two things: (1) to achieve a specific result and (2) to avoid hurting the other person's feelings in the process. Assertive behavior seeks a win-win outcome unlike aggressive behavior that seeks to achieve a specific result at all cost and to extract an emotional price from the other person by insulting or putting him or her down in some way. It is not always easy to be assertive but learning to deal with problems in an assertive, constructive, and appropriate way is essential to your success on the job.

Dealing Effectively with Criticism and Manipulation

Constructive criticism is most likely delivered as part of the feedback you receive from your employer during formal or informal performance reviews. It is important to know how to handle such criticism, by knowing how to respond correctly, as well as by remembering what not to do. The sole purpose of criticism is to assist us in improving some facet of an existing situation. In order for the criticism to be helpful, both parties must create an environment that encourages candid communication.

Preparing Yourself for Criticism

The most common situation where we face criticism is in the performance feedback discussion. It is essential that we gain a complete understanding of what the employer is saying so that some appropriate corrective action can take place. There is an appropriate reaction to criticism and it involves asking questions until you have a very clear understanding of exactly what the criticism is all about. When dealing with criticism ask questions to gain clarity, do not make excuses, do not become defensive, then respond in a professional, confident manner by asking how the person would like to see the problem or concern resolved. Learning to accept and learn from criticism is an important aspect of being a professional personal assistant.

Growing Professionally

Developing professionally generally requires furthering your formal education and your employment experience. You have two choices in growing professionally: the first is to do it right where you are in your present job; the second is to look for opportunities elsewhere. When seeking professional growth in your current job, get the employer's consent to do more significant work and assess how much time it takes you to complete those new tasks. One of the best opportunities for growth is to ask to do those tasks your employer puts off or avoids doing.

Personal Computing

Technology has indeed changed the way business is done. The internet helps us find information in a snap and PDA's are being converged with mobile phones and digital cameras. From one sole device, PAs can now search the internet; place phone calls; lookup contact information; write to do lists; and send email. Internet access is no longer limited to dial-up connections or even DSL; there are wireless access points (sometimes FREE) at hotspots locations around the US. You can locate these services using one of the directories below:

- http://www.wififreespot.com
- http://www.lessnetworks.com

As the reliance on technology continues to expand, the role of the personal assistants has greatly evolved. Office automation has led PA's to assume a wider range of new responsibilities. PA's are responsible for a variety of administrative and clerical duties necessary to run their employer's lifestyle efficiently. They serve as an information manager for a home or office; they plan and schedule meetings and appointments, organize and maintain paper and electronic files, manage projects, conduct research, and provide information by using the telephone, postal mail, and e-mail. They also handle travel arrangements. A thorough understanding of Personal Computing is crucial. Assistants are aided in these tasks by a variety of office equipment, such as facsimile machines, photocopiers, and telephone systems. In addition, they use personal computers to create spreadsheets, compose correspondence, manage databases, and create presentations, reports, and documents by using desktop publishing software and digital graphics—all tasks previously handled by outside companies or service professionals. The internet can be used to find information on just about any subject these days. Before embarking on a career as a Personal Assistant, one should find a training center or local college that offers courses on computer and internet basics.

Case Study: Assistant on the Go

Once settling into a new position, one of the first things an assistant does is organize her office. From her personal workspace, she completes tasks using her computer; answers phone calls; manages her boss's calendar; sends faxes and more. The true measure of star PA is whether she can work outside of a traditional office environment.

Sandy landed a new job as an assistant to a television producer. She worked from his office and was exceptional at managing his lifestyle and business needs. She was extremely resourceful and always managed to beat deadlines. One day she learned that she would have to work on-location with him in Canada for a new television project. When they arrived, they spent the first few days working out of a hotel prior to setting up their satellite office on the set. Whenever her boss gave her tasks to complete, she panicked. She felt like a fish out of water without the "system" she was accustomed to, although the hotel has a fully functioning business center. Once the satellite office was set-up and she had her fax machine, phone line and computer set-up on her desk, things were smooth again. Once the project ended, her boss informed her that she needed to learn how to use technology to enable her to work from **"anywhere."**

Public Relations Savvy

More than likely, your employer will have a professional publicist at his disposal. However, it is still imperative that you understand at least the basic functions of public relations. There may come a time when you will have to assist with drafting a press release to convey information about a project that your employer is involved in.

One of the first things you should do when you start to work for a new employer is to forge a relationship with the media in your area. Call the broadcast journalists and producers at your local television stations and invite them for lunch or tea. Do the same for print and radio media personalities.

Below you will find fundamental information regarding how to write and distribute a press release:

What is a press release?
A press release (also called a news release) is a document issued to the media to announce a product, partnership, event, personnel announcement, or other newsworthy item. Editors, reporters, and journalists depend on press releases to alert them to unique products, trends and changes in the business landscape. Press releases, normally written by a public relations professional or by a PR firm, are delivered to journalists and analysts for review. If the journalist or analyst finds the announcement of value they may contact the 'subject of the press release' for more details and/or an interview. This may result in being mentioned in an article or broadcast.

How do I write a press release?

For an announcement to be considered newsworthy it must have a broad, general interest to the target audience and a strong news angle (e.g. material information, new development, drama, human interest, local angle, consequence, etc.). In addition, your release needs to be written in a journalistic rather than marketing style. It should be objectively written as though a reporter were writing the story for you. Most importantly, your release needs to "inform" people, NOT just sell them something.

Headline Formats

In most cases your headline is the first thing an editor sees when reviewing your release. An effective headline can make a difference between an editor covering your story or hitting the delete button. To create effective headlines consider the following pointers:

- Limit your headline to no more than one line. Many newsrooms have a limit on how many characters they can receive in a headline and their systems are programmed to "bounce out" releases that exceed this limit.

- The headline should provide an editor with a tantalizing snapshot of what the press release is about. This is critical as many journalists view releases over their wire system by headline only, then pick and choose when they want to view the full text of the release.

- The headline should include the name of the company/person issuing the release.

- Do not include the terms "Company", "Incorporated" or "Limited" or their abbreviations unless they are necessary to clearly identify the organization, i.e. Entertainment Corporation vs. Entertainment Brands.

- Do not use exclamation points or dollar signs.
- Attribute all potentially libelous, critical, controversial, or judgmental statements.

Writing Style Requirements

Writing a professional and effective press release can be difficult. Here are a few guidelines to consider when crafting your release:

- Get to the point quickly and back it up with quotes and evidence.
- Use proper grammar and punctuation. Check for typos, and don't just rely on spell check!
- Address who, what, when, where, why and how in the press release.
- Double check phone numbers and URLs.
- Read your release aloud to see if it makes sense.
- Include quotes to convey opinion or affiliation.
- Don't forget to put your contact name, release date, dateline, web site URL and phone number in your release. Also make sure you are available for phone calls after sending the release out.
- Your release should be written objectively, as if the writer has no affiliation with the company or person the release is being written about.
- Do not use pronouns such as I, we, us, our, your, etc. except in direct quotes. Write in third person.

- Do not use puffery statements or hype (i.e. we make the best widgets East of the Rockies), but do inform the reader of your status in your industry.

- Always include standard boilerplate information about your company in the last paragraph. The headline for this section should read "About (insert your company name or the person the release is being written about - here)."

Length Requirements

Your release should be concise and to the point. You should be able to convey your message in two pages or less. Releases that are less than 50 words in length tend to be advertisements and cannot be run as a news release. If you are going to use bullet points, use them sparingly.

When should a press release be issued?

A press release can be used to announce a variety of information. Consider the following examples:

- New project (starring in a new film, recording or releasing a new album)
- New product (starting a clothing line, perfume, etc)
- Significant modification to an existing product
- Changes in corporate identity, such as company name or logo
- Joint venture
- Features
- Events (golf outing, speaking engagements, award ceremonies)
- Philanthropy (volunteer work, donations)

- Hiring of agencies (public relations, accounting, law firm)
- Media advisories

Distributing Press Releases

There are numerous services that will distribute your employer's news worthy announcements to a targeted list of media sources quickly, accurately and affordably. Consider these resources below:

- http://www.prweb.com
- http://www.prnewswire.com
- http://businesswire.com
- http://www.ereleases.com

Event Planning

"From celebrity hosts at Sell-A-Thons, to celebrity appearances at walk-a-thons, to usage of celebrity Masters of Ceremony, the stars are an asset to any fundraising endeavor —- and an automatic lure for media coverage of the event.

As objects of popular culture and consumption, celebrity persona can be used to mentor, to lure monetary relief, and to motivate Good Samaritans from all walks of life to respond. In fact, according to studies by the Independent Sector, a philanthropic collective, most people start donating time or money because of direct appeal of a personality they can identify with. Further studies show that Americans believe celebrities can help unlock the door to the media for social causes. Three out of every ten Americans surveyed say there are not enough celebrities helping worthwhile causes in the media.

Celebrities, executives, and civic leaders set examples. They can also sway public opinion in ways that save and transform lives. More fascinating figures that glare at us from the headlines are discovering that leaving a blueprint for a better civilization is the ultimate act of leaving ones' mark. More profound than winning a championship game or an election, receiving a Grammy nomination, or achieving multi-platinum record sales is bequeathing a tiny piece of self." – **excerpt from Shining the Spotlight on Celebrity Goodwill - By Regina Lynch-Hudson/The Write Publicist & Co**

As a personal assistant, you may have to coordinate your employer's participation in fundraisers and other special events. You may also have to plan events and parties. To do so, you must understand the basics of event planning:

1. Determine the type of event.
2. When would you like to hold the event?
3. Where would you like to hold your event?
4. Consider the details such as catering, entertainment, guest lists, etc....

Travel Industry Knowledge

Personal Assistants spend a lot of their time arranging travel. At any given time, your employer may embark on an extensive travel schedule; from business meetings to parties to special events to premieres to movie sets to family vacations to tours to media interviews.....

You should get to know the sales managers in cities frequented by your employer. Become very familiar with their favorite hotel, the type of rooms they prefer and the amenities they expect upon arrival as well as any special needs. When assisting the family with planning their vacations; be sure to research major cruise lines and their fleets, private facilities and homes for rent in exotic locations and private air charter.

Your knowledge of the travel industry is vital. You should make a concerted effort to understand:

- International Travel
  - o Passports
  - o Visas
  - o Entry Requirements
  - o The State Department's role
  - o Health Considerations
  - o Customs
  - o Returning Home
- Cruise Ships
  - o Major cruise lines and their fleets
  - o Cruise areas
  - o On-ship facilities
  - o Cruise features
  - o Food – drink - Entertainment
  - o Communications to and from ships
- Domestic Travel
  - o Accommodations
  - o Recreation
  - o Special events and conferences
  - o Transportation
  - o Food and beverage
  - o Airline terms
  - o Types of airlines
  - o Types of aircraft
  - o Airline seating arrangements
  - o Private Charter
  - o Airport Lounge Access
  - o Hotel Industry Terms

Security and Logistics

Your employer will have personal security, executive protection/ bodyguards; it is important for everyone in their support staff to still be cognizant of the basic skills of protection. Providing security means protecting items that belong to people and to their property. *You* are a key part of your property's security system. For example, you can watch who comes in and out of the property, and you can look for unusual situations.

When it comes to personal security, it will be helpful if you take courses in executive protection as well as seek instruction in some form of martial arts. Below are some resources:

http://www.trojansecurities.com

http://www.esi-lifeforce.com

http://www.ipg-protect.com

http://www.inxtec-security.com

According to the polls, fear of crime is America's number one concern. Naturally, this has caused a multitude of businesses to jump on the bandwagon, hoping to profit off of those fears. Locksmiths, alarm companies, karate schools, security companies, weapons manufacturers, guard dog kennels and so on, all promise us the security we need to survive these troubled times. The professionals in the protection field, whether police, military or personal protection specialists, understand that security is a multi-dimensional discipline.

Training for personal assistants can be provided in everything from firearms to martial arts, but in order for it to be effective; the training must be part of a complete self defense system. There are basically three stages of personal protection, each requiring a certain degree of preparation. These stages are awareness, avoidance, and defense. All three are part of a system and need to be approached as a lifestyle if it is to be an effective system.

Awareness means having the ability to recognize possible or real threats as well as the ability to anticipate the unfavorable conditions that are conducive to an attack. In protection work, a lot of emphasis is placed on the advance team identifying potential threats so they can be neutralized. So it must be with your own protection and the protection of your employer. It is your responsibility to become educated about your surroundings.

Avoidance is the next logical step in your protection arsenal and frequently the one that is ignored most. Many assault victims report having a "bad feeling" just prior to an attack. Whether through advanced planning or a "sixth sense", we should be able to recognize potential threats and avoid them.

If, after taking as many precautions as possible, we find ourselves under **attack**, we must make a multitude of decisions in a very short period of time. Do I resist? How do I resist? Is retreating an option? Is compliance an option? Do I have the skills and ability to defend myself? When we make the decision to fight back, it is absolutely necessary to be as dynamic and powerful as we possibly can be. There is not the luxury of sparring and attempting to "temporarily incapacitate" our attacker. One very effective way to prepare for an attack is to visualize the most frightening situation you can imagine. Let your mind create the entire scenario, from initial attack to the only acceptable conclusion; your survival. Do whatever it takes to survive and don't let doubt cause you to hesitate. Without taking self defense seriously, you are like an ostrich who hides his head in the sand and hopes the danger will pass. That is not personal protection; that is giving up your right to self defense.

Household Management

Although we have focused on the professional skills and personal attributes of a successful personal assistant; we will close with some of the traditional services PAs must offer. Management of an employer's household is part of the PAs role. Depending on the employer, an assistant may share this role with the Household Manager or Butler. You can save time and become better organized by creating a system to assist you with keeping track of information regarding your employer's (and their family's) activities, contacts, schedule, etc. This can be done in the emerging way, with technology tools such as a personal digital assistant (PDA) or using a reliable system of forms and files to organize and manage information needed to run the home. Sample forms are included in the **Appendix B** to use as a guide for developing your own Household Management system.

Concierge Services

The skills outlined in this book can be used to start a business supporting a group of clients – rather than one high profile individual. Personal Concierge and Errand Running Services are a much needed resource for business owners, the elderly, new mothers and many other time-pressed people. Time is fast becoming the 21st century's most valuable commodity. Almost everyone's daily life, not just celebrities is jam-packed with work and domestic responsibilities. Yet extra hours in the day are something money can't buy. Or can it? An affirmative answer comes from a variety of local and national entrepreneurs whose burgeoning services add up to what can be called the "don't-do-it-yourself" industry.

Dionne M. Muhammad

Appendix A: Author's Picks for *on-the-go* Tools

Personal Digital Assistants:

Blackberry PDA Phone

The Blackberry offers wireless email, calendar and contacts management as well as synchronization with Microsoft Outlook. The Blackberry also supports web-browsing.

Wireless Internet Service:

Verizon

Verizon Wireless' national wireless Internet service enables users to access the Internet, corporate email, attachments, and business applications with a laptop without the need for dial-up, T1 or DSL access.

Printing:

PrintMe

Print or fax anything, from any device, everywhere you go. No cables, drivers, or complex set-up. PrintMe is simple to use, secure, and lets you get the most from your wireless technologies.

Computer Remote Access:

Go To My PC

GoToMyPC allows you to remotely access your computer from any other Internet-connected computer in the world with almost any operating system through a secure, private connection.

Fax Services:

eFax

eFax provides Personal Assistants and other mobile professionals with a local eFax number to send and receive faxes.

For more information about these tools, visit:

www.celebritypersonalassistants.com/patools.html

Dionne M. Muhammad

Appendix B: Household Organization Forms

Weekly Schedule

Monday				Tuesday	
Number	Name			Name	Number
		9			
		10			
		11			
		12			
		1			
		2			
		3			
		4			
		5			

Wednesday				Thursday	
Number	Name			Name	Number
		9			
		10			
		11			
		12			
		1			
		2			
		3			
		4			
		5			

Friday				Saturday/Sunday	
Number	Name			Name	Number
		9			
		10			
		11			
		12			
		1			
		2			

Emergency Contact Information

Travelers

Name	Date of birth	Passport number	Other identification

Airline Itinerary

Date	Airline	Phone number	Flight number	Departure city	Destination city

Hotel Itinerary

Date	Hotel	Hotel location	Hotel phone number

Lost / Stolen Credit Card or Traveler's Check Information

Credit card type	Issuing bank	Credit card number	Phone number	Name on card

Traveler's check type	Value	Check number	Phone number	

Dionne M. Muhammad

Away From Home Checklist	☐			☐
Stop newspaper	☐			☐
Stop mail	☐			☐
Stop deliveries	☐			☐
Notify police	☐			☐
Call alarm company	☐			☐
Make pet arrangements	☐			☐
Notify neighbors	☐			☐
Unplug computers/phones	☐			☐
Unplug appliances	☐			☐
Turn off hot water heater	☐			☐
Shut off gas	☐			☐
Adjust/turn off sprinklers	☐			☐
Empty trash	☐			☐
Shut off water to icemaker	☐			☐
Shut off water to washer	☐			☐
Check stove and oven	☐			☐
Water plants	☐			☐
Close drapes and curtains	☐			☐
Set light timers	☐			☐
Adjust thermostats	☐			☐
Set security system	☐			☐
Lock house	☐			☐
	☐			☐
	☐			☐

Daily Diet Tracker

Food	Serving Size	Calories	Servings By Food Group						
Date : _____			Grains	Vegetables	Fruits	Dairy	Proteins	Fats	Extras
Notes : _____									
Today's Total									
Compare to Goal									

Daily To-Do List

To Do:	To Buy:
To Go:	To Call:

Family Contacts

Name:	Phone:

First Aid Kit Checklist

1 box small adhesive-strip bandages	☐
1 box large adhesive-strip bandages	☐
1 box assorted sizes adhesive-strip bandages	☐
1 box nonstick sterile gauze bandages, assorted sizes	☐
1 sterile rolled/flexible bandage	☐
1 box sterile gauze pads	☐
1 box triangular bandages	☐
1 sterile bandage tape	☐
safety pins	☐
disposable latex gloves	☐
scissors	☐
tweezers	☐
eye wash/eye cup	☐
small splints	☐
1 box bottle syrup of ipecac	☐
antiseptic spray or lotion	☐
burn ointment	☐
aspirin/non-aspirin/ibuprofen pain reliever	☐
Anti diarrhea medication	☐
calamine lotion and/or hydrocortisone cream	☐
small plastic cup	☐
thermometer	☐
hot-water bottle	☐
gel cold pack (keep in freezer) or plastic bags for ice pack	☐
small paper bag (for hyperventilation)	☐
emergency contact information with phone numbers	☐
quarters for pay phone	☐
first-aid guide or book	☐

Dionne M. Muhammad

Shopping List

Date	Store	Brand/size	Price	Unit

Travel Packing Checklist	☐		☐
Underwear	☐	Toothbrush/paste/rinse	☐
Bras/T-shirt	☐	Dental floss	☐
Socks/stockings	☐	Brush/combo	☐
Pajamas/robe	☐	Hair pins/scrunches	☐
Bathing suit	☐	Shampoo/conditioner	☐
Beach cover-up	☐	Hair spray/gel	☐
Tops	☐	Perfume/aftershave	☐
Shorts	☐	Nail care items	☐
Pants/skirts	☐	Soap/shower gel	☐
Dressy outfit	☐	Razor/ shaving cream	☐
Sweater/sweatshirt	☐	Deodorant	☐
Jacket	☐	Moisturizer/lotion	☐
Casual shoes	☐	Aspirin	☐
Dress shoes	☐	Allergy/antihistamine	☐
Sandals/flip-flops	☐	Prescription medicines	☐
Hat	☐	Glasses/contact lens	☐
Sunglasses	☐	First aid kit	☐

Weekly Menu Planner

Week of _____

	Breakfast:	Lunch:	Dinner:
Monday:			
Tuesday:			
Wednesday:			
Thursday:			
Friday:			
Saturday:			
Sunday:			

Dionne M. Muhammad

Appendix C: Further Reading

It's All Your Fault: Adventures of the Hollywood Assistant:
by Bill Robinson, Ceridwen Morris

Fab Job Guide: How to Become a Celebrity Personal Assistant
by John C. Havens

Be a Kickass Assistant - How to Get from a Grunt Job to a Great Career
by Heather Beckel

Building a Partnership With Your Boss
by Jerry Wisinski

The Devil Wears Prada
by Lauren Weisberger

Threesome: Where Seduction, Power and Basketball Collide
by Brenda L. Thomas

Organize Your Office : Routines for Managing Your Workspace
by Ronni Eisenberg

File...Don't Pile : A filing system for personal & professional use
by Pat Dorff

The New Executive Assistant: Advice for Succeeding in Your Career

by Melba J. Duncan

Order these and other great titles online

http://www.celebritypersonalassistants.com/training.html

Celebrity Personal Assistants, Inc.

Los Angeles:

1800 Century Park East

Suite 600

Los Angeles, California 90067

Office: 310-407-5163

Fax: 209-396-3543

Atlanta:

1230 Peachtree Street, NE

Suite 1900

Atlanta, Georgia 30309

0ffice: 404-942-5728

Fax: 404-942-3757

New York City:

245 Park Avenue

39th Floor

New York, New York 10167

Office: 212-672-1933

Fax: 646-304-2439

www.celebritypersonalassistants.com

info@celebritypersonalassistants.com

About the Author

Dionne Mahaffey-Muhammad is the President/CEO of Celebrity Personal Assistants, Inc., (CPAI) a staffing agency that exclusively recruits and trains business-savvy Personal Assistants for celebrities and professional athletes. The agency has offices in Atlanta, Los Angeles and New York. During the initial launch of CPAI, she toiled as an assistant for an NFL family. Previously, she worked in senior management at software and engineering firms. She frequently lectures on topics such as "Changing Careers;" "Women in Business;" and "How to Balance Home and Work," among other topics. She lives south of Atlanta with her husband Charles, a software quality engineer and their children Charles III, Ashanti and Nasir.

CPSIA information can be obtained
at www.ICGtesting.com
Printed in the USA
BVHW031754090519
547822BV00003B/65/P

9 781418 466718